Additional Praise

TARTA AMERICA

"In *Tarta Americana*, the celluloid and actual Rit[...] body double and secret sharer, the shape-shifting [...] ...u walks us through the cloaca of the political present and media sphere, through our unlived life in the industries of desire. Ritchie Valens's 'We Belong Together' in the key of My Bloody Valentine's *Loveless*. Ritchie Valens as Rilkean angel and Orphic repository. Ritchie Valens as the recipient of a centerpiece epistolary sequence that further proliferates into many-sided embodiments ever larger than life—the 'story-shape' exuberant and relentless in Martinez's quest to integrate what was broken or torn apart. The sonic register spans from the caustic vision of Mexican folk balladry with its existential *vacilada* to the custodies of *ixiptla* as presence and making present, and the maximalist cascade of 'one more nonlinear, / sweat stained star- / lit night pulsing / police lights / across the rain-streaked / windshield where / our most furious / apprehensions / blur all Rothko red.' . . . *y arriba y arriba*." —Roberto Tejada

"'Flying guitar, what we knew is you flew,' says the speaker in J. Michael Martinez's dazzling, book-length riff—code-switched—of Don McLean's iconic song, lamenting the day the music died. Yes, Martinez deploys his signature array of formats and linguistic registers, only here his focus is one Richard Valenzuela aka Ritchie Valens—a brilliant epistolary lens, through which the poet offers his most personal and vulnerable poemario to date. . . . We are movingly persuaded when, in the end, the poet says: "These pages /are my hands, / you're holding / my hands."" —Francisco Aragón

"Ravenous, cinematic, lost to angsty doldrums of rollerblading 'past / Hollywood Video's rows / of Styrofoam VHS dreams'—this is *Tarta Americana*, a love letter. Martinez craves a deeper connection, past the iconography of a talent who died tragically and too young: the further Martinez 'scrape[s] the narrative' from his own skin, the more something more intimate than the myth of a man emerges, something 'outside time, ear into the soft, it is *this* emptiness I want: our sacred outside existing only in each other.'" —Rosebud Ben-Oni

"Ritchie Valens, immortalized for 'La Bamba' and 'Donna,' dead at seventeen in a plane accident, is here both patron saint and proxy-self, and *Tarta Americana* is both bildungsroman and protest song, a story of family and love, of the pain of growing up, and wide-eyed witness to the casual racism that culminates in cruel violence. In poems that pulse with a lyricism so bright it borders on the technicolor, this gifted poet gives to us what poetry and song have given him: 'twin consolations to the noise.'" —Dan Beachy-Quick

ALSO BY J. MICHAEL MARTINEZ

Museum of the Americas

In the Garden of the Bridehouse

Heredities

TARTA AMERICANA

◆

J. MICHAEL MARTINEZ

PENGUIN POETS

PENGUIN BOOKS
An imprint of Penguin Random House LLC
penguinrandomhouse.com

Pages 127–128 constitute an extension of this copyright page.

LIBRARY OF CONGRESS CATALOGING-IN-PUBLICATION DATA
Names: Martinez, J. Michael, 1978– author.
Title: Tarta Americana / J. Michael Martinez.
Other titles: Tarta Americana (Compilation)
Description: New York : Penguin Poets, 2023. | Includes bibliographical references.
Identifiers: LCCN 2023010173 (print) | LCCN 2023010174 (ebook) |
ISBN 9780143137115 (paperback) | ISBN 9780525508625 (ebook)
Subjects: LCSH: Valens, Ritchie, 1941–1959—Poetry. | LCGFT: Poetry.
Classification: LCC PS3613.A78644 T37 2023 (print) |
LCC PS3613.A78644 (ebook) | DDC 811/.6—dc23/eng/20230616
LC record available at https://lccn.loc.gov/2023010173
LC ebook record available at https://lccn.loc.gov/2023010174

Printed in the United States of America
1st Printing

Set in Garamond 3 LT Pro
Designed by BTDnyc/Beth Tondreau

for Dante, Talia, Tyler & Trinity

for the many infancies—
surviving within us,
surviving despite us—

so love's eternities
may   at last
blossom & hold

CONTENTS

I

II. LETTERS TO RITCHIE

III

TARTA AMERICANA

I

You're mine and we belong together.
Yes, we belong together, for eternity.
                    —Ritchie Valens, "We Belong Together"

Sally Sparrow: I love old things. They make me feel sad.
Kathy Nightingale: What's good about sad?
Sally Sparrow: It's happy for deep people.
                    —*Doctor Who*, "Blink" (S3 E10)

[VEILS THRU VEILS, THOUGH FACE SHEARED, YOU CRUSHED TO ME]

for Adam Toledo, killed by police in Chicago, March 29, 2021
for Ritchie Valens

Bent to pavement, blacktop, brown face, skinned knee
in the narrow where fallow shadows grip
Veils thru veils, though face sheared, you crushed to me

Did fame flay you white for white fame's white need?
Name knelt, name split, what price for white conscript?
Bent to pavement, blacktop, brown face, skinned knee

I've knelt for the belt, scourged, nail gun to cheek,
ash sweet, ass beat, blood slick, a brown convict
Veils thru veils, though face sheared, you crushed to me

'fore iron entrails crushed, outside quiet strings,
spring's flesh unfolds gold wilds—must we forfeit,
Bent to pavement, blacktop, brown face, skinned knee?

Far from shore, we swim the pale death sings,
those solar cries, what lovers lies restrict,
Veils thru veils, though face sheared, you crushed to me

Croon & take, wake the roses flesh graved, we
are here, buried & bound, a star's relict
Bent to pavement, blacktop, brown face, skinned knee
Veils thru veils, though face sheared, you crushed to me

[YOU'RE]

—We Belong Together

an ANGELLO FABRICATION

You're your brother Mark, you're your cousin Jorge, you're sitting in your parents' garage, & you're the rusting car motors scattered around you, & you're sixteen swigging Budweiser 40s, souring your tongue with Gold-schläger, & you're thirteen, as Jorge says, "Our name is Martinez; fuck everybody else, Cuz"; & you're your brother raising the bottle to your lips, gushing fluid gold down his throat, & you're the butterflies bursting from the liquor, thrusting your wings through your breath, & you're his words crawling into the air like wet wings, "Familia, bro, that's all that matters," & you're a cliché but later, you're the police pulling your brother from your cousin's car as your brother falls facedown to the concrete, & you're his arms twisted over your head, your shotgun to your temple.

Hair like an aurora sheen, strands
as he turns in libidinal dance,
guitar in hand, rhinestone sparkling
star-spangled peonies where his utopia
had been, but now, only a hollow

heart punched into ribs, he dissolves
holding a smile as savagely tarnished
as memory, perhaps, as desolate & lost
in pleats as if Alzheimer's collapsed
the blue sublime behind him;
if not for the cannibal skies,
he would always sing under
what sows the shadow
his death sews for smile.

It was night. Shadowed. The lone road to the colonia deserted. Each petal. The miles from the city. Where they slept. Outside its limits. Nothing. Past the sand yard, past its fracturing. Unutterable. Over the bridge. Curve. Past the Poudre River. Homecoming. & she ran. Sorrow-grazed. From the lights not there. Masquerades. She had been walking home. The Arches. To the colonia. The truck had passed her. Only minutes ago. Terror begins. In smiles. She saw their lights. Heard its horn. Disappear behind her. Boundless. She heard tires. Squeal the day. But no lights. No love in dew. She ran. To open. Into the dark. Spring. My mother ran. Off the road. For gully ravage.

It was 1966

The world wasn't. Into the ditch. Into element. She hid. The path. Lay in the mud. Looking up. For angels. In the moonlight. She saw. The pulsing. The vulture's stark. Headlights dark. The black in white. The men roll. To a stop. Mirrored in her. Twenty feet. From her. She hid. In daughter dance. Among fescue overgrown. Fibers green. Long hairs for lock. For rescue. Grows dim. "She was just here," she says she heard the window say. Closed. They searched. In fleshwater. Incomprehensible. For twenty minutes. My mother obscured. & remained.

Never the song before the movie.
Always that crying guitar
twining. Around a monochromatic sky.

As *Lou Diamond-Ritchie*'s recurring
trauma childhood dream
unwinds. Airplanes

over a schoolyard. Where he wasn't.
& never witnessed. Brown children.
Uniform slick, cinematic tell-all flashback.

Black & white slack
shorts. With ankle-high
white socks hitched in contrast

with a darker gray
calf. Playing ball on the blacktop.
& the silence. As the sky

burned. White shadows
down on white slack white.
But after *Lou Diamond-Ritchie* wakes,

just before the *fade*
to black, the guitar cries
its keen circular closure,

around a monochromatic sky.
So I witness a brown boy
who can't speak Spanish,

will world a word
a chorus to cry.

◆

Whenever the song,
it's never just *the* song. It's Los Lobos.
But it was never just Ritchie's either.

Never just one-color,
it was already everyone's
when *he* sang it.

& I'm eight again.
When the guitar's pluck
skips, flirt-like

hesitations before the slide
down. & round again.
& I'm dancing on the table.

At Fonta's pizza parlor. Where
we're all sitting, the five of us,
Mom scowling one second, then

all chuckle clapping in the joy of it,
breadsticks served, I jump down just
before our "American" (mushroom,

pepperoni, sausage) pie is served
in Technicolor, singing, *Por ti seré,
por ti seré. Por ti seré, por ti seré.*

TARTA AMERICANA

Child, fuck Ted Cruz.
　　　　　—RuPaul, *Jimmy Kimmel Live!*

Bob: Look, man: *"Ritchie Valens."* With a name like that,
nobody's even going to suspect you're Mexican.
　　　　　—Luis Valdez, *La Bamba*

O' beautiful streams of halcyon
skies, we drove YouTube memes
through Upstate Karens
all the way to another deep-
fake's purple majesty,
through Wyoming's statewide
anti-kale/pro-tourism campaign
(like kale gives a Wyoming-fuck),
past Salt Lake, giggled Honda halos
on the salt flats before peaking
in Nevada, an ace & king
in hand as we spindle-spend
& fold, at last, into the South Bay,
& on the first day of our first life
in San Jose, working under
the hood of a '64 Chevy
Chevelle parked on *our* driveway,
fortune found us one
shirtless *La Bamba*,
neck & torso tattooed,
& Corona in hand;
after handing me a bottle,
he says, in Afghanistan,
the lieutenant's
limp tongue led
his platoon with an
ignorance one VHS
rental wide, thus, *Barrera*
was branded *La Bamba*—
from *Valenzuela* to *Valens*,

all the broken colors,
pop song to Hollywood,
now, to name-stripped soldier—
any brown commodity
that is, boy, for rebranding
will do—& in a Bob-less
brotherhood, *La Bamba* says
he shot his gun singing sea
to shining sea, *Then conquer*
we must, when our cause it is just,
& this be our motto—
"In God is our trust,"
& *La Bamba*, the former
soldier, not the song,
now jobless, homeless,
&, after four tours,
linguistically fracked,
says he feels kinda hollow
stateside, seems like
everyone's meme-life
is chasing childhoods
that never were;
& then, with a nod
we slap hands,
& swig our bottles
back, & *La Bamba*
slams the hood down,
with an *adios*, he drives off;
I haven't seen *La Bamba* since,
but I listen for him, singing,

Bye-bye, Miss #Amerikkklan Pie

I want to tell *La Bamba*,
in the '90s we rollerbladed past
Hollywood Video's rows
of Styrofoam VHS dreams,
past the pastel sunrise
arching over McDonald's,
Walkman blasting, "Today is

the greatest . . . ," everything
all honeydew, Sunday fireworks,
but today, in 2022, on Insta,
everyone's shaving their ankles
bloody like a machine
in service of the state,
dancing the cucker
in loops, & after, wanting
thicker ankles, I-280's
obscure exits lure *me*
out for *you, Tarta*
Americana, neon red pulsing
black impermanence,
your potholes, a kind of heartbeat
I feel I'm inside, the tent camps
lining the chain-link fence between
another organic honey-butter
sunrise cream & a day's worth
of dumpster-diving plastic
Pepsi eyes trenched in
the grime blind, singing,

Bye-bye, Miss #Amerikkklan Pie

Tarta, remember when every exit was
an ocean lullaby wash, endless waves
of traffic shush & squeal,
through the budding limbs
of apples, orange, peach, & fig,
trees riper than traffic life,
carpenter bees buzzing
drunk like another man
shamble-ranting off the exit to 10th Ave.,
the 7-Eleven, sprawl oasis, every Twinkie
coconut sugar fluff crumb gathering
spiders, dried twigs wheat bright,
& starlight, star bright,
O' Tarta, hear my wish tonight,
is this the one
where *I'm* the spear,

& *you're Jehovah* raising
tablet & testament, carrying
civilization from the wheel
to your own Mecha
pulverizing cities.

#Amerikkka, your lies bloat me
empty; really, I know I'm just
an ash-caked doe
washing my scalp
with knobbed elbows,
my hooves too awkward
for the froth & bubble
to get clean, again, & you,
#Amerikkka, tar drunk, were waiting
to conquer your ninth New York,
history can be what
you want it, when you own the program,
the conditions & variables,
intelligence, vigilance, & violence,
more conditionals for your pleasure,

Bye-bye, Miss #Amerikkklan Pie

#Amerikkka, history could be
more than your self-pleasure
& you see my mother
at seven crowned in pearls
of bloody sweat, draped
in her older sister's hand-me-down
dirty gray dress, picking grapes,
onions, & lettuce with penitent hands
that whisper to the plants
the color of her children's eyes,
#Amerikkka, I taste her prayers, she sang
"La Bamba" to rosary beads.
Her Hail Marys & Apostles' Creeds
on my tongue,
overflowing my mouth,
& she's singing "La Bamba" from outside

time & it is me my mother has bled
& my name is *Tarta Americana*
for this ain't no son song
of a *Martin* smoothed *-ez*,
sweep into the brack,
the brine left
in the water's black
echoing out through your
pupil—there, you'll find me,
the girl-follicle left
after the promises
held in the lips parted lisp,
unteachable, untranslatable,
this Mart turned Tart
Tarta Americana
papel apple
pie soured
fifty years dead,
living *La Bamba*
decades before
another Martin
saw *that* mountaintop
& another Martin
peaked the dance
charts, queerly, everyone
Livin' la Vida Loca, that is,
America, as *Tarta*—
my doe spine folds
under the black for
oil rainbows, not the hush
after the shotgun, but for asphalt
shushed, I-80 to San Francisco
& the city, street by street,
avenue by avenue,
exits freeways onto freeways
down & behind my left eye,
a migraine, all static
& gasoline & snarl-spit
pulsing one more
popporn redemption,

savior story: all white,
blue, & red-pleathered,
#Amerikkka, stop/don't stop
screen-grabbing me
grateful, feed me
my new *historical*
sex cream, & *#Amerikkka*,
if my safe words are *green card*,
#Amerikkka, this picnic
blanket's for you,
& if you promise me,
every fantasy contingent
to hunger, *#Amerikkka*, as one body,
we'll refuse *"our future"* every instant,
swear me I'll milk the crow's tongue,
spindle-spent, torch flung
for a less violent love,
but, *#Amerikkka*, today,
tarred & feather-boa'd,
kidnapped & caged,
these wings have founded
strife as a kind of love,
no dualities, just
the *tar* of tartare
for delicacy blood raw,
but, *#Amerikkka*, you keep ordering
tart steak à l'américaine,
a frank file smelling rank
egg & no yolk
sunrise over the crowds cheering
as a Tanned Rump rallies
against another ten-flush toilet;
culture flushed,
fifty stars staked
to your Red Hat;
#Amerikkka, call me
Tarta, I'm *We* flung
to the drain,
all natural *Asco, Asshole*
mural born shitstain

art à l'américaine,
#Amerikkka, our name is tar
& you drive my face's tear-
marked tarmac
up my mouth & take
exit U.S.C. 1325
down our children's
ambient screams
as we turn through
Tarjorie Gaylor Mreene's
mouth when she kneels,
& "prays" for one more
performance artist
in his self-made prison, crying,

Bye-bye, Miss #Amerikkklan Pie

O' *Stupid #Amerikkka,*
tar me splendid
one more pandemic
spring's pink spume:
hips as light
as blush petals
cherry blossoms twerking
post me spread-eagled
as I stream my next heart
attack, don't worry, Jake
Paul'll DM you
a steepled ambulance,
a custom Kardashian
to style your cheeks
messianic; O' *#Amerikkka,*
you're up past the curtain
call in first class, taking it
puckered personal,
that tourist demanding
a hot towel,
& hand job with peanuts,
& beside you,
the Great Orator

bent on riot shields,
licks his finger's
Kentucky sauce:
he's President Spread-Eagled,
he's tax-lean, & he's just
buried his ex
to the side
of his first hole
trimmed green, & he's swinging
the smallest iron,
smacking his balls
all red, white, & orange,
21st-century Republicanism
the Tonald Drump Manly
festo destiny: one youngster,
every two years eaten
by the bigger beaks
whose leathery wings lumber
folded, diggin' in
like a blue knee
to a brown throat;
& *we* stare, all cigarette butts
scattered across the sidewalk
like clipped fingertips, singing,

Bye-bye, Miss #Amerikkklan Pie

#Amerikkka, my sweet freedom
hole lives in teeth,
& on Florida & 7th St.,
#Amerikkka, you see *me*,
Americana tarting,
as pigeons light from bare branch
to leaf-shaped cinder block
& I'm that homeless
broken beer bottle
staring from the gravel
as trash collects in the gutter
like discarded conversation
saying, *water, tea bag, needle,*

saying, *glass, baby bottle, refusal,*
so, *#Amerikkka,* after years
of the burger burp messiah
waxing off on Fox
about erection fraud,

after night after night
of choking down
one more Cucker
Tarlson, all crotch-light
in a testosterone tizzy,
nipples harder than nails,
edging toward the end
of another monologue,
moaning, *The Great Replacement,*
Mexicans are rapists,
Chicken Wings are People,
& that pedophile Peter Pan
buying pizzas from Democrats,
emailing Neverland
from Hillary's email . . .

Truly, *#Amerikkka,* aren't you
cuckered out yet? Isn't it
time to tuck it in & sing,

Bye-bye, Miss #Amerikkklan Pie

Tarta Americana,
I'll tuck it in for you, *#Amerikkka,*
tight between my thigh's
Love Island, taped around my
raw bottom for
all your red-ribboned hero
quests sung white,
lipless virtue
cock hard, Snow stabbing
Dany, all the dragons
cash splashed flaccid

for one more fatherless
Boy-Man whose Christ lips
Christ awed, whose tongue,
oyster raw, ousted reason
total Trump-tan tweeting

Citizen redneckkked   *in desperate dilly*
white rally   *blue dramaloo*

rats mirror-starved
mirrors rat-carved

open   *the gods*
inside your   *fuck-star*

Passive pie crust stuffed
voyeurs, *#Amerikkka*,
don't worry, I love
you watching me watch you
as, *Tarta Americana*, we bleed, spiritual drill
to the meat, & its sweet bouquet,
the zero petal opening its thorn, singing,

Bye-bye, Miss #Amerikkklan Pie.

Chorus sung, voyeur rose rung,
#Amerikkka, when the complicit have tossed
their flowers, & cheered,
who, in the end, departs the grave?

Not the dead.
#Amerikkka, who's earned
the coping ladder
out of trauma's deep?

The tourist or the tortured?

Don't answer, *#Amerikkka*,
don't think, just start
tarting *Americana*,

with bell-bottoms ringing,
we're destined to the fiber
between, sacrificed without
our deaths, *Americana*, our fiber
& flesh shear original love eyeless,
all we shattered animals—
the *we-children* between—but not only;

#*Amerikkka*, love moves the world
from our deaths, & to tart,
we propose an amendment
for immediate ratification:
shear love from the fiber,
the many sounds god bore,
#*Amerikkka*, we many must
separate love from between the flesh—
we rabid gardens, we lanterns
shattered & turned to tendon,
#*Amerikkka*, forget essence,
we children through veils & between,
#*Amerikkka*, we children spectral
the most promised hymn, but not
only, under our eyes, we exist, but not
only, angel-stretched, & budding—

America, before the picnic,
pedestal our deaths between love
& strife—meet me there,
the most simple smiles
tearing our faces together,
just two nowheres, singing,

Bye-bye, Miss American Pie.

you have so
many names
for, not only,
names
you don't see
the way
my brain sees
you
see
my brain
sees colors
in a different way
as
I hear
the browns the blacks
the blues the reds
the pinks the whites
all the sounds
the colors
make my brain
hear
so many
not only names
for
the browns the blacks
spectrums
you don't
color
all the names
my brain sees
my don't-names
blue the reds
the pinks the whites
you don't know
how many times
my skin
has been

pink the brown
my skin
sounds
my brain
so many
names
sex
a different way
all the brains
you don't know
in
the sounds
the colors
skinned
the browns the blacks
the blues the reds
the pinks the whites
the browns the all
my name spectrums
your skin sounds
skinned
has been
my skin
how many times
you don't know
the pinks the whites
blue the reds
my don't-names
my brain sees all the
names color
you don't
spectrums
the browns the blacks
for
names
so many
hear

I hear
the browns the blacks
the blues the reds
the pinks the whites
all the sounds
the colors
make my brain
hear
so many
names
for
the browns the blacks
spectrums
you don't
color
all the names
my brain sees
my don't-names
blue the reds
the pinks the whites
you don't know
how many times

ALL THE LUSHNESS SUMMER WALKS

Dear Ritchie, all the lushness summer walks,
you sing, & still, *love* only ever encroaches
suicide starfuel—Romeo & Juliet's brightest *Hollywood*
&, there, in the gravities of our isolations

sunrise sings, "Shall I compare thee," &, "My Mistress,"
lovers of such gossip, fucking each other purple,
a kind of slain star—the *Hollywood* skyline's brightest,
&, Ritchie, everything is a lie & it's all true,

such gossip, lovers fucking each other *Purple
Majesty* for all our vanity's wax melt wings,
&, Ritchie, we're all the same kind of slain star:
fingertips, & panic-attack text messages,

all our mirror's wax majesty, a Hollywood
skyfuel's brightest star panic-attack
sexting, Ritchie, *Fuck all the summer lushness,
fuck all the slain lush   summer stars stride.*

In the distance, across the litter of rusted & skeletal Chevrolets, peat-shit-spotted chickens, miniature tornadoes harvesting the dust of empty plots, the parameters of bloodstained barbed wire, standing as a monolith refusing the rows of trailer homes with broken wood stairs leading to doors with hinges rusting like vertical eyes, an ancient maple tree's branches had, in spring, fiercely erupted its emerald wings &, now, was an oddity: an earthbound jewel held to the endless tan plain.

The boy, leaning against his uncle's white truck, stared at the tree. He listened to his uncle Valentine & grandfather talk. Here, in the plains of Colorado, his grandpa barely subsisted on his retirement. The old man lived alone in his trailer. His sons would visit him infrequently. Rusted engines, in various states of disarray, littered his yard like abandoned & decayed bison carcasses. Regret seemed to be the only other living thing besides the weeds. The boy wondered if he would end up alone like this.

The boy couldn't understand their Spanish. They spoke too quickly. His uncle, sooty brown skin etched with smile wrinkles, was a roofer. He had hired the boy for the summer &, now, after the morning's work, he wanted the engine he had brought to be fixed. He would sell it to buy back the nail gun he had pawned the week earlier to pay his family's bills.

The seventeen-year-old boy was exhausted: he woke daily at four a.m. to the honk of his uncle's beat-up pickup, then worked for eight hours until the sun beat him into a sweaty pool, hammer hanging from his hand, iron nails poking into his thin gut from a workman's pouch. He wiped his face with his white shirt &, looking at it, saw streaks of mud.

The boy watched the dust gather force, willing itself into spirals. One dust cloud arose at his feet, sweeping onto the road & toward the distant maple. He imagined the small twister was a ballet dancer pirouetting streaks of white over the staid earth. She pointed to the tree, beckoning & promising.

When he came to, the boy was already a few trailer home plots away from his uncle & grandpa. He looked at them, their already small figures, his uncle towering & strong, cheeks sharp like edges of obsidian; his grandfather was hunched over, whiskey-brown face deeply creased, skin sagging, bushy white eyebrows, & peppered hair, & gnarled hands crossed in front of him as he leaned on a wooden cane for support.

Despite his hunch & the need of the cane, his grandpa towered over his uncle with his coal-black eyes. The father & son were still *the* father & *the* son, time had not eroded authority from the body of the old man as it had from the steel of his home, the grip of his hands.

The boy turned toward the tree. His uncle Val & grandpa would be talking for a long time yet. He had time. In the distance, the tree became a promise. If he climbed it, he would ascend into the clouds & would dance as ballerina. If he could only get a single green leaf, it would be a ticket to another world. If he refused the leaf, he felt the rust of the engines, their empty frames unable to power any vehicle, would come for him.

The boy started walking. The tree was a dot in the distance, but it looked as if the road ran directly to it. He began to daydream. In his mind he saw a single crocus growing: as seed, it knows only heart. A tendril of green root pushes through shell. It pursues the earth for nutrient. From nutrient, the seed is told the original history of boundary—the earth to sky, the sky to sun: how the earth, newly made, longed for the love of the free-willed wind. Newborn, it didn't comprehend the limit of gravity, the endlessness of space from which it had been framed. Unknowing, it sent its heart to the sky. Lost, the earth's heart mourns to the earth's soul, tides receding & returning in foam, love's gift causing the ocean's turmoil. The black seed, knowing only the crusted womb filled with worms & of the eye turned to world, now filled with the mystery of love, reaches down & up toward the limit. Surfacing, the green arm wills itself into fisted bud. There, the night air caresses the tucked newborn. Withholding, resting in itself, the unborn is told the myths of light. Hearing, desiring this unknown, the bud pushes its roots further toward the earth, stretching into the voice of its origin. At dawn, the fist will relinquish & spread. Feeling light within its most tender folds, the crocus blossoms. Roots holding tight, haloed in the spectacle of the sun, the once-seed surges into a thousand hues of saffron. Wind tells the tides the endlessness of the sky with life. The blossom, for the first, endures the love that tears into birth, eternities of communion screamed into its belly.

The boy did not think these words, he saw these images. From these images, I imagine him thinking, "We chalice actors act our chaste silence, we chaste waves begging chalice for shore."

But the boy didn't think this.
The boy thought of his loneliness.
The boy touched his cheek's pimpled blossom.

A torn scream, then growling.

Tensely standing ten or so feet away on the side of the dirt road, a bulldog slavered & snarled. It yelped & pawed a step forward.

The boy took a step back in fear. He backed away slowly, forgetting the tree. When he looked away from the dog, he saw the tree was much closer than he remembered, only four or five trailer homes away.

The boy turned to the dog. Was it worth being bitten by a rabid dog? The boy thought about his life, the pride of his grandpa's hunched figure, his uncle telling him he had to pawn the nail gun but they would use hammers to finish the roof & use the money from that job to buy back this essential tool.

The boy faced the dog, its watery red-beaten eyes. It growled, brown teeth bared against its bleeding gums.

The boy took a step forward.

The dog lunged.

With a sharp *ping!* a chain snapped, & the boy snapped his head back. The dog gave a pitiable yelp as its body continued forward with momentum, the thin wire collar strangling it. Retreating as the boy passed, the dog barked fiercely but its force was castrated by the collar.

Not turning, the boy listened to the dog as the tree before him stared down at them. The leaves were a bright & luscious cream-green, branches heavy & weighed down.

But then, a deep growling.

Turning from the tree, now only ten or so feet away, the boy saw a mutt, across the road from the tree, rise from where it had been resting in the shade beside a trailer home. It yelped, baring its rotten teeth.

The boy looked for the dog's collar.

The mutt paced the side of the road, panting & snarling. There wasn't a chain or collar restraining the dog.

The boy searched the dirty windows of the nearest trailer: beyond the dirt-crusted glass, broken white blinds were shut against the midday sun. The punctured screen door was shut, but within the shadow, the boy saw a black-and-white TV snowing static.

The dog paced back & forth like a panther. No world in its eyes, just the boy. It snapped its head up & down as it yelped.

Glancing up at the tree, the boy stepped forward, not running but searching for a low branch to climb. He would get bit, he knew it. As the dog leaped, the boy, out of the corner of his eye, saw a blond streak.

"Stop!"

The dog, skidding to a stop a few feet away, turned its head & whined.

Frozen, the boy turned to face the piping voice. A blond-haired child, wearing dirty cutoff jeans, gestured to his feet. The mutt, head bowed, whined as it went to the little boy. Topless, the little boy's white chest & arms were covered with scratches & crusted mud. As the dog sat before him, the little boy kneeled, petted it, & stared his hard blue eyes at the stranger. The boy, standing still, felt those eyes accusing him like a finger in the chest. He, against his own will, started to walk, needing to flee from the child's unforgiving gaze.

A minute later, as he approached the tree's base, he heard the unmistakable jingle of his uncle's rickety engine. He reached up & plucked a single leaf. The familiar horn blared.

"What the hell are you doing?" his uncle's basso voice called behind him. The boy turned. His beloved Uncle Valentine, one arm draped over the open driver's door, stared at him.

"Are you crazy? What the hell were you doing? Get in, I gotta get you home & then come back here. Boy, you must be crazy!"

The boy held the leaf in his hand. As he climbed into the truck's cab, he pulled out his wallet.

"Michael, I don't know what is wrong with you! I swear, god dammit," his uncle said, shaking his head.

The boy placed the leaf delicately into his wallet, trying to avoid folding the small green leather. He said to his uncle, "Thank you for picking me up."

[MINE]

—We Belong Together

an *ANGELLO FABRICATION*

A strand of black hair holding as luminescence that does not want to die; *The Book of Laughter & Forgetting, Invisible Cities*; a face firming into your cheek's smooth ovals—two unhurried wings; both of my deceased grandmother's rosaries I wear for every reading; my belief, taught to me by my grandmother, that everything, from mineral to animal, resonates with meanings *of* & *beyond* a sight that

will not be
owned.

HIGH SCHOOL SUMMER NIGHTS:

& we lay on the trampoline,
staring past our confessions
to the stars bridging all
the distances between lips.
Proof: I still own the mixtape
that began my A-side life,
where every beginning echoes
the Cure's "Pictures of You"
under the mistletoe,
while you jab
your emerald sharp
fingernail into the mouth
of my whereless castles.

Leather-worn now,
as the speakers pound,
the valentine retears
my tears, & I sing-scream
one last cupid wing
for one more nonlinear,
sweat-stained star-
lit night pulsing
police lights
across the rain-streaked
windshield where
our most furious
apprehensions
blur all Rothko red.

[SUDDENLY EVERYTHING'S ALL 1999]

Suddenly everything's all 1999
in 2XXX—Prince & André 3000
& violet bruised eyeliner
& black nail polish
& my nylons torn
ass grinding against
another stranger's firm
lifetime of regrets
I've always had junk
in the proverbial
& in a skirt
I'm always all cherries
floating in vodka & coke
a splash ready to leave
one more dry martini

But what if, tonight,
this look-alike
demon-slaying Dean
Winchester
was my Rilkean angel,
unholy enough
to fuck my leaves
sun-milk sated,
& under his gin
& cleft chin,
holy enough
for my thighs to rest
beneath his language,
safe, circled in salt
from the demons
of our own making,
& what if, in *that* circle,
another kind of demon
took hold, & it had nothing
to do with what was holy
or sacred, but with how

we could be one sacrifice,
& what if we let
what we could keep
holy play us   all 1999
Prince & André 3000
& a new year's bruised eyeliner
& black nail polish
& our nylons torn
ass grinding against
another regret's firm
cherries promise-floating
in vodka & coke?

IXIPTLA (9) TLAZOLTEOTL, THE FILTH EATER

The blossom growing from the heart is small, a seemingly insignificant
detail, & yet it is the flower of redemption, for the goddess Tlazolteotl
tells us that we are all worthy of her forgiveness.
—Chicome Itzcuintli Amatlapalli, *Mi Corazón Mexica*

Lady Filth Eater,

> fold me—a *once-upon-a-time* scab-boy
> with pale breasts
> > & marble bones,

> at nineteen, a slice of white peach
> across the bed frame,
> > face scarred into hunger,

> a baby scooped lipless,

> & my days passed in afterimages
> laid clear before the blur;

My Lady,

> fold me—in fishnets & mascara,
> I swallowed
> > eyes like almonds,

> face powdered for pretty,
> > carmine lips lipstick languid,

> I squatted nude over a bowl of milk
> > on a mirror

> > to lure my altar boy,
> > > to boy my altar lurid.

&, my Filth,

eat me—& I'm seven again,
below the splash for the first abuse

in the rec center pool,
wearing wet translucent white

swim trunks when the swimming
coach, a sixteen-year-old

girl,
took me to the end

of the pool to teach the frog stroke,

the breaststroke;
facedown,

legs moving as if gathering the water
to itself, my arms parting the water

before me, the movement of propulsion:
to gather & divide; she held me up, afloat,

with her right hand, the soft warmth
against my clavicle;

with her left, she reached into my shorts
&, fingers clenched in fist
around my question,
murmuring, "Do you like it?"

Enfolded,   Enfolded,
Lady Eater,   Lady Filth,

I don't remember   I remember

the gasping for air
      my fear   to reply to touch;

            the next day,
            crossing the crosswalk
            to the rec center,

the asphalt
      tar became gutter gray,
my body trembled,
      & the world's colors

imploded, television static all,   blinking snow

          consumed trauma's form,
          a thousand hammers

          clanging

          a scream fingers cling
          as I listen through the purr

                to the teardrop
                growing the grape.

     & fold me,
     my Filth,

        innocent again,
        as pretty as an altar girl—

           my skin, my face

           a noose I'd knot

           for bow & cream.

           My skin folds in & out,

static the stagnant fold,

Lady Filth Eater,

fondle my nouns furious,

fiddle me
in skirts,

skin scarred into pretty,
for I pale the scars in powder,

peach-lit
& leech-lipped

to suckle
any noun's pout.

ADHD FAIL OF THE WEEK

& Thursday,
all neon-blue leotard
        legs nylon'd,
            pink headband
                wrapping my hair
            in a bow called *Santa*
        as I fill up the tank,
slipping on my heels
            while my roommate opens
        the door with a splash
            of cake across
            one more dog's

            anxiety-ridden howl,
            & I try, again, to get myself
                out of the swing without

                    the fire department,
                    but even if I wanted,

                    even if the bicycle
            would make it across
            the thin plastic
            bridge, the pizza's
                    already slipped

out of our hands,
& somehow, we still think
we're the singer in this rock band,
but I've been dragged drunk across
the sidewalk singing Journey
too many times to forget
the size of the stage,

or that curb I always hit
that rolls my car,
or that I'm too big for high chairs
when I slip walking across
that iron beam called heartbreak,

& when I drag husband down
off the stage for a kiss,

flesh handled into one more strip
dance in front of   Grandma,

it's like the time
the crocodiles raced
to leap at my own stupidity,
but, Baby, I know there is no courage
in a selfie while the serpent
spirals the tree,

& yes, the elephants

scare me, because, even here,
        the anacondas

        slip through the glass

door every time we put my *me*-baby to sleep,
my story-shape all swallowed jawless.

LSD ORPHIC DISORPHISM

My LSD Orpheus, / before you / & after you
lovers wild—paradise / birds—spread their
claw dance / against solitude / for anchor;
before you / & after you, / lover's brevity—
acrobat balancing / on no sunwise string
of cartilage / from which dangles all

the angels, / a virtuosity all
want & weight, / a puppetry without, / & you,
Ritchie, / song lit, / defy the string,
& sound—one organizing star, / youth's
symphony / in the brevity
of all we want: / a hand to brave the anchor

grounding our hunger's patterns. / Love, what human core
was holy? / A "citizen," / but my pigment / a noose; awe
the masters, / & images / patrol love's brevity,
desire cords / as crook'd / as question / marks around you, & still, / even
lynched, / dew evaporates. / I had the strength, / once, to imagine /
freeing myself from me, pluming

thighs conjoined, / flesh, nerve, / & marrow plumed,
& us, luminous, / stars fucking halos.
I fancied raising anchor, & escaping / what I live, / what is
inside us, / the string behind the veil, / soul freed / of such
distension, / all of myself given / to you; identically / altered, me
in you, we, / mirrors of a thousand gasps; if brave, / I'd tie

my left / hand to your right, / my night to your song's / brevity
so the road / behind my shame / would lead, / plumage
at last wingless, / past the lower worlds, / past you,
through the sky / of no / one's eyes, past / the anchors
in the sickle / shape of your face, / where we would
plant all heal, white / blushing to violet— / we would string

out over eternity, / in bushels, / the null-gift strung
into the botanical, / our flesh, the meat-crown / of this brevity,

& this wound, / too, / would become joy / in the denial left,
after all / is offered, / this practice of love / & betrayal, plumes

   torn, rib-lungs / meat raw;
   from my chest, I'd carve anchors
   hollow to hold / only our death,

   no-time outside you.

[AND]

—We Belong Together

an *ANGELLO FABRICATION*

Maria Jesus Martinez & Jerry A. Martinez; Jerry & Mark Martinez; Mark & Ivan Martinez; Ivan & Dante Martinez; Dante & Talia Marie Martinez; Talia Marie & Tyler Martinez; Tyler & Trinity Martinez; Trinity & Tiffany Martinez; Tiffany & Josh Martinez; Josh & Sonia Martinez; Sonia & Gabriel Martinez; Gabriel & Uncle Luis Martinez; Uncle Luis & Aunt Rachel Martinez; Aunt Rachel & Uncle Valentine Martinez; Uncle Val & Uncle Ramon Martinez; Uncle Ramon & Jessica Martinez; Jessica & Jennifer Martinez; Jennifer & Emily Martinez; Emily & Aunt Janie; Aunt Janie & Uncle Frank; Uncle Frank & Aunt Lupe; Aunt Lupe & Aunt Carmen; Aunt Carmen & Uncle Pete; Uncle Pete & Uncle Joe; Uncle Joe & Uncle Ignacio; Uncle Nach & Matthew Ross Thomas; Matthew & Adam Taub; Adam & Carmen Giménez; Carmen & Andrea Rexilius; Andrea & Eric Baus; Eric & Mathias Svalina; Mathias & Jeffrey Pethybridge; Jeffrey & Carolina Ebeid; Carolina & Patrick Pethybridge; Patrick & Sommer Browning; Sommer & Rosebud Ben-Oni; Rosebud & Vincent Toro; Vinnie & Grisel Y. Acosta; Grisel & Aaron Angello; Aaron & Sophie Staires; Sophie & Erin Costello; Erin & Mark Rockswold; Mark & Lacie Cunningham; Lacie & Chris Haynes, &&&&&&&

II. LETTERS TO RITCHIE

You know, you don't have to give that to the audience.
They haven't earned that from you.
You do not have to give them your ways of coping;
that is for us to hold as our own safety.

—Jennifer Koh, quoted in Joshua Barone,
"Two Musicians of Color Are Creating
Their Own Space,"
The New York Times, April 8, 2022

I.

Dear Mr. Ritchie Valens,

Yesterday was your birthday, so I loop-played "Donna," my headphones
cycling your croon seducing soft as I walked to the post office, but after
crossing the train tracks, just before the fifth time *you roamed alone*, a
rambling truck, rusted forest green with rims & bumpers paradoxically
polished to mirrored perfection, slowed as it passed, & in the cab, three
teen *Chads*, shoulder to shoulder, eyed me, & one with a blond buzz cut
leaned out the passenger window, grinning gap-toothed, & said
something, but all I heard was you, Ritchie, "Since she left me . . . ," &
then, the teen waved a small Trump/Pence 2020 flag, but by that time
you were calling out to Donna like she was Eurydice, & while the teen
flipped me off, I was wondering if Donna was your first *real* love, so I
guffawed smilingly at him as I remembered my first crush's name,
Rhonda, as if every first love's name rhymes with "-Na."

Ritchie, the Trump teens drove off pandemic summer laughing just as an
afternoon rain began, & listening to you, walking in the downpour that
afternoon, I wondered if the oceans tally the rainfall, adding up what's
necessary for union. The death tally yesterday was 6,198.

Maybe between our deaths, love is just that, a precipitation
process—a sky refusing the stagnance of noon until everything is in
tears, &, Ritchie, I remember *that feeling*, you know, when your chest
chains all the lightning? I had just turned seven, & that April, in a
valley bordered by pine & aspen, its grassy field cut cleanly through
by a thin stream, I remember, the morning shining down on this
field dotted with thousands of dandelion cypsela, cottony seeds
rising behind me as I brushed my hands across those stemmed
stars, & as those seeds took flight, I remembered, Ritchie, my
mother telling me if you could catch a single wisp, you could incant
a wish, & yes, at seven, I believed in magic—nothing since has
changed my mind—& I remember running through that dandelion

field, its trillion seeds exploding into the air, &, Ritchie, I admit, I'm a
sappy doll, & I thought of *Movie-You*, how *Movie-Donna*'s *Movie-Father*, all
MAGA-minded circa 1959, kept *Movie-Donna* from seeing you, Ritchie,
so *Movie-You* sang "Donna" from an empty, midnight phone booth on
some empty street corner, &, Ritchie, watching you in that phone booth,
you, singing through racist surveillance, of *this* world alive, revolutionary
with dandelions, floating seed clouds, & silver coins beneath a mountain
water so pale it was almost the clarity of snow.

II. (THERE'S NO WAY TO KNOW THE *YOU* LANGUAGE EXPLODES INTO)

Ritchie,

There's no way to know the *You* language explodes into, yet *Movie-You* always begins in flashback, already seventeen, but dreaming of where you never were as a child: over a crowded school playground, a saturated, chromatic-trauma frightmare where two planes slow motion crash. Ritchie, snap to black, *Movie-You* gasps awake & upright in bed, let me tell you, Ritchie, I've flashbacked upright in bed too, where *Younger-Me* thinks, "Waiting for the party to end, who remembers the music?"

But it was Dead or Alive—"You Spin Me Round (Like a Record)."

It was June of 1996. The endless red. Plastic cups. Beer stink & flirting. A balmy night, sticky sweet like nervous hands. Time a small distance then. The lengths round our wrists. & the night was nearing the witching. The hours passing in sigh shadow, hiding my pained paint face behind long hair. Bottles of laughter foaming. & I'm the narrow corridor. Now. We go out back to the patio. To play hacky sack. I want to leave. But the hacky has been thrown. Right foot cradle. & there are four of us. The hack spirals up, twirling yin-yang leather. Always judging. The objects. We kick.

Always the twirling. Justice like a ballerina. & Ryan cradles it in the crook of his foot pausing balanced on one leg. & again, it arches up, smiling between dusty pairs of sneakered feet.

&, Ritchie, in memory, we never stop playing the balance game. Hacky.

But we are. Walking through the alley. Summer dusts. The darkness. My hands are in my pockets. & we're turning right, to the sidewalk in front of the house. To the car parked a few cars' distance. From that crowd spilling over the sidewalk into the intersection. Like a herd.

Of pinballs.
& snap.
A car crackles. Gun Pop.

&, Ritchie, I remember him shallow running. A gunshot gazelle in slow
motion. Out of the crowd. A swift blue blush. Blurring a body radiant.

Holy is the distance nowhere in memory. Holy the smiling dust the
summer crackles.

& our camera zooms. His face a small. No. In memory. There is only the
flesh blur. The outline of color. Hands moving. As if to unbutton. His
chest. His fingers touching. Memory.

&, Ritchie, he's always. Dilated eyes at me. & the gas station's neon.
Filters the cool smell as if it had just rained. & this world's mushroom.
Drunk, & two words. Shimmer crystals, Cocteau Twin chorales. Shatter
pure my sound-memory. Two words. Of the stillness of themselves. A
kind of

     sonic folding

     akin to higher synchrony.

"Help me."
"Help me."

III.

Ritchie,

In *La Bamba*, when all your *Movie-Family* gathered, I remember I loved
seeing all the brown bodies—they looked like my uncles, aunts, my
grandma & grandpa—& I remember, Ritchie, how, in *La Bamba*, near
the beginning as we're introduced to your brother, when we're on the
tarmac, & the camera zooms down the road from the POV of Esai
Morales's *Bob*, pure leather-clad rock & roll straddling a Harley. That grin
& nod he tosses *Movie-You* before you embrace, & then, just after, dozens
of brown mothers, fathers, brothers, sisters congregating around a bonfire
as you play guitar:

that sense of familia—for the *first* time in my young experience, in
movies, at ten years old, gawky, bucktoothed, with glasses as thick
as Buddy Holly's, I found resonance, a mirror to my '80s
childhood—that clustering of star-filled nights of music &
mixtapes, vinyl records & rhythms, that music a familia makes
when living *the love* of a familia, Ritchie, you know, it's like the
palpitating wires off a subwoofer, a heartbeat pulsing down my
network of memories, there is the sound of laughter & tears, the
husky moist of the steam off the brisket, &, beneath long black
eyelashes, the quiet stare of coal-black eyes as my six maternal
uncles sat with their spouses, all generous with a gentle wit & softer
smile—eyes always alive with a child's wonder—recounting the few
days since we all last saw each other, as they plan ice fishing in
Wyoming, & all the while, my three maternal aunts, & their
spouses, my mom, these wisecracking sisters, gamble cards (*Follow
the Queen*, of course), my grandma looking on, all tapping their feet,
shoulders swaying to *your* syrupy strum, Ritchie, as you sing "We
Belong Together," sigh-throbbing from the speakers of a small
Sony beatbox on a foldable table beside the chips, salsa,
guacamole, & a tin of tamales steaming up there, in the back of the
garage, in shadows behind, deeper shadows spilling out into the
backyard, my innumerable cousins, closer than most brothers &
sisters, running through the ink-black but fenced-in grassy
backyard, joking & fighting, fucking up shit, then making up &

hugging after being scolded, always stepping over some cooing
baby,

Ritchie, it felt like running through a late spring evening of floating
dandelion clouds, wind whipped up & sunset lit under a background of
peach-soft purple clouds spilling down like watercolors onto my parents'
laughter—it felt like those nights would last an eternity into the ripe
sunrise breezing through the garage's rusted brown hue.

IV.

Ritchie,

It's been sixty-four years since your body was found covered by February
snow in a stubble field. Pointed south, face buried in a white drift, your
crushed skull may have been a compass to Huitztlampa, the place of
spines, where the energy known as Huitzilopochtli resides, the solar
palace where that manifestation issues demands of human sacrifice. But,
Ritchie, you were never Tenoch-Mexica (Aztec). You were a teenager from
California. You weren't sacrifice. Ritchie, you were a victim of an ill-
begotten flight. Or maybe, Ritchie, you *were* sacrifice. Your body cast to
the earth, so that your music could remain, here, crying for the love you
never had the chance to begin.

It's been twenty-seven years since Daniel Waltz's body fell to the ground
close to the corner of 16th St. & 14th Ave., a small hole piercing through
his shirt, sternum, lung, & heart. Pointed south, his head turned to me, I
remember his eyes magnetic with shock, as he said, "Help me." His
whisper, the relaxing dilation of his pupils, are a compass to me, guiding
me to a solar palace where a young man, still twenty, has fulfilled all his
life goals, & now listens beyond his death to the pure music behind
unfettered belief. He wasn't a sacrifice. He was a victim of an ill-begotten
shooting. Or he *was* sacrifice, body cast to the dirt, his unmoving pupils
dilating still in my memory, haunting my purpose, demanding the
fulfillment of dreams he never had the chance to begin.

[WE]

—We Belong Together

an *ANGELLO FABRICATION*

The almanac begins by taking it, permeating it, easing it onto the ground, where intimacy embraces sighs with juices coursing from root through stem into fruit, where spirit is synonymous with the body, where night mirrors the call, & the heart, at last, moves desireless where we hang lynched by the rose, strung from the arms of the child once in us, our listening laid reverently upon our chilled tongue like a wafer, & at last of eternity, our mouths permeate, sounding the bell, scattering the seed, & we, abandoned, hang as chapels before the abyss, a marker to gaze beyond & embrace; our heirs will swing beside us, brittle vessels filled with oil & mirror shards whose depths reveal pearls grinding to dust, fruit rotting to seed, the celestial within the stone fruiting arms that stretch out from our corpse like a child that reaches up to embrace its mother, the merest ring wrought of fool's gold, worn on the finger, permeating the void through our carcass, a metal sunrise we must embrace.

V.

Movie-You begins waking from a recurring dream.
Foretelling of your own death;
Movie-Me begins sleeping after recurring self-
awareness. *He* couldn't be saved;

& *Movie-You* said, *I wasn't there when it happened.*
But in the dream, it's like I am;
& *Movie-Me* said, I was there when it happened.
But in the dream, it's like I'm not;

& *Movie-You* said your BFF *Got crushed by one of*
those falling planes;
& *Movie-Me* said his BFF was crushed to his
knees. By the one fallen on the grass;

Movie-You said, *You weren't at school* that day.
Said, *You were at your grandpa's funeral*;
Movie-Me said, *His* eyelashes—long, brown, like
mine. Said, I'd never attend my own funeral;

& *Movie-You* said, *I guess his death saved my life*;
& *Movie-Me* can't speak. We write. *His death didn't*
save our life. But we can. See-swoon it;

& *Movie-You* said, *My mom says it means I was saved*
for something special;
&, Ritchie, my mother never says that to *Movie-*
Me in my *Movie-Head*;

but I promise, Ritchie, when it's the summer of
1996 again, & all the blisters of July collapse gun-
shot across our palm, *Movie-Me* will movie you all
of Valentine's guitars, an orange-

sherbert, VHS-sunset replayed raw, Ritchie, my *no-*
you as awe, I promise, no more cigarette burns
will ever bracelet our summertime wrist,
&, Ritchie, all life closer, we'll kiss until rewind.

[BELONG]

—We Belong Together

an *ANGELLO FABRICATION*

I remember holding the cassette tape, & tearing off the cellophane wrapper. I remember the smell of the newly printed paper insert, its chemical warmth. The first time I heard My Bloody Valentine's *Loveless* was on a Sony Walkman FM/AM WM-BF59 cassette player: I was walking home from [_____] Central High through a late October snow, the first or second of late autumn, when all the still-falling leaves, burgundy crisp, have yet to mulch these brittle wings, musky mute ambers & blotched crimsons bursting across the snow-gray sidewalk like blood vessels across an eye's shadowed white.

VI.

After your stepfather   passed, Ritchie,
you were sixteen, sweat-stained bandanna brow-
bound, when you started picking the fields in the
opening scenes of *La Bamba*, & like you, my family
worked the fields, my mother, uncles, & aunts
caravanned state to state as infants, one of a host of
families my grandpa led after returning to Laredo,
Texas, to fulfill the bargain he'd made with farm
owners strewn across the states: origin of DIY,
Martinez-inflected punk ethos, however, my
maternal grandfather is a mystery to me; my mother
refused to speak with him for decades after he
abandoned one family, hers, for another early in her
teens; imagined loyalty wants me to imagine him as
less anti-immigrant than pro-Martinez (an
immigrant himself), but I don't know; the story
goes he pledged he & his would provide "better"
labor than the braceros or undocumented labor *if the
farmers would agree to his prices*, & the farmers, having
worked with him, having trusted & relied on him,
hired him. Contracts in hand, he gathered a train of
border families, & they'd picked fields, paid fair for
fair labor, & one morning, my uncles tell me, after a
visit to the city, driving back to camp in their black
1950 Chevy pickup past fields of lettuce, of squash,
my grandpa slammed the brakes
      & skidded to a

              stop
              in
front   of   my   grandma,
&   he   stepped   out   flourishing
a   record   player,
a few 45s in a paper bag, &, Ritchie, that night,
my mom says her little brothers built a bonfire,
& my grandma made tamales, & she says she

danced *to such lovely sounds*, arms raised, six years old,
cotton dress as innocent as Communion wafers,
& she says she & my aunt sang up to the stars
beside the rows of green that, the next day, they
would   reap,   but   this   night,
spinning   like   a   record   player,
they   twirled   to   your   "La   Bamba,"
& I see the stars caught in that cyclone
of song & skin, spiraling faster & faster down
past fire & dance, into their eyes, songlights
past   bone   &   gene   until,   Ritchie,
you stepped through them, foraging childhoods
for   the   many   infancies   a   smile   may   sing.

RITCHIE & BOB

Twinned in horizontal
stripes, a thatched fence & house

whose wooden white
twin doors dilate

pallid repulsion over
the children, more predator

than home, more swallow
than womb. The older behind

the younger; Bob, choirs against
his belly, the grass yard at angles

where little feet danced & fell,
&, Ritchie, you're an infant

in the obscurities of a frown, or
in first step, that delight,

a brother caring for a brother
more non-dual urban paradise

for non-dual jukebox jeweled
sacrifice than any heaven's threshold

VII.

Ritchie,

It was *after* Daniel Waltz, *after* watching his pupils seek their last words, *after* having tasted & swallowed the blood flooding his lungs, coughed up from the bullet wound, it was *after*, that following weekend *after* his death, hiking far into the woods with an older group of high school kids who'd witnessed the shooting, including my best friend's older brother, RT, who'd performed rescue breathing & CPR alongside me, who'd years later become a fireman, who'd, after the ambulance & the police arrived, held me as I *truly* cried, so unlike those tears noosed to my embittered garage narcissism, tears welling up from the unexcavated depths of all the deep images unsung within me, crying from *not* understanding a violence that could crack through to the labyrinths buried within everyone's morality, from having faced a face vital with life as it dilated into *that most known unknown*; Ritchie, it was when RT & I, having breathed for this twenty-two-year-old, having compressed his chest together, as I'd been taught in Boy Scouts, working his heart as it stopped working for him, rescue breathing for him after he'd stopped whispering for help, after he stopped coughing up blood, the red like some watery lipstick on his paling face, his blood still on my lips when, *after*, Rodney pulled me close, the first hug I'd received in so long— because hugs hurt me, Ritchie, always bursting any number of cysts across my chest & back, let alone my face, the reason all my shirts are black (not to be cool—rather, pragmatic)—& a few days later, it was deep in the Rocky Mountain National Park, the weekend after Waltz's death, staring up at a thousand stars flaring through carmine stellar gas, purple-hued galaxies, that I saw a mystical riot of color, all undiminished by the brilliant hazed glow of the moon, that I traced that sky brilliant with such beautiful constellations, those myths ranging across known space, that I thought about the night before Daniel's death, when I'd held a noose tight in my hands, reflecting on what my mama, my dad, my brothers would've found in the garage if I'd climbed that ladder; &, Ritchie, I thought of Daniel, having heard that he had been saving money to return to college in the fall; it was *then*, Ritchie, staring up into that narrative sky traced from stars, likely long dead, those constellations casting stories Daniel would never ponder again, it was *then*, Ritchie, I made a promise to *him* whose heart-pulse I'd swallowed, I swore to strive for every distant constellating dream I'd ever spun out of my own human distance, that I would love as deep as those deep images I'd cried, I swore I would find joy in this tenuous threshold called my body for as long as it could rescue breathe; &, Ritchie, today, I've learned there is no distance between longing & loss, that the work of memorial is never complete, that our eyes are always full with the unapproachable relentless, that there are limits all kissing must accept, & that our pupils dilate wide to swallow all these vivid expanses of conclusion.

VIII.

Ritchie,

My love for *Movie-You* was because it showed, to my child eyes, a
"Mexican American" "artist" for the first time, a method to comprehend
why. We so long for narrative. Some place to lay our head. To place this
engagement, this moment, this immediacy into fictional refraction. Yet,
Ritchie, there is so much unknown about the *Living-You*.

Yet, still, relinquished, the *Living-You* remains.
                              One silver crucifix.
                              One religious medal.
                              The numerous receipts found
                              languaging in our pockets. When
                              the morning clips itself.
Inside the tongue, Ritchie,
& our pink longitude quiets.

Yet, still, those two-sentence obituaries
of those relinquished to COVID, Ritchie, & each story, no matter
how brief, burns.

In the practice of this story,   Ritchie,

                              we must first study the heart:
                              four prayers
                              with two roads,
                              four doors, & one body:
                              a chamber without word
                              where first principles gain flesh

&, when fleshing out the myth, Luis Valdez said, the flesh was still miss-
ing you:

The problem is that Ritchie had been dead for thirty years, & he was a cherished memory. Nobody wanted to say anything bad about him . . . "yeah, he was a nice guy, nicest guy who ever lived." I kept asking, C'mon, didn't he ever do anything wrong, he must have been human? . . . I wanted to know, Did he ever get laid, did he do drugs, how was he human?

Ritchie, time is so slow, & so long & so persistent, & we sacrifice such common bruises to unlearn ourselves, our monsters laying eggs in our berth as they feed on the corpses we make of the heroes we hope we will be.

Yet, Ritchie, this universe. Such luminous redundancy. The emerald thousands. In each shoal. Ritchie, there was so much

Living-You never did; just as your hits "La Bamba" & "Donna" were topping the charts, you were gone, only seventeen.

Ritchie, what would the *Living-You* say to *Movie-You*? Would you be proud? Did Bob really take you to see a curandero in the mountains? Did you really eat snake? Just below the cloudline, in a narrow Oaxacan valley, between mountains, a curandero found *me*, wandering the cornfields, fed me chocolate his wife made—from the milk of her goat, from the cocoa he grew. Maybe every mouth is a hungry myth?

So, Ritchie, *of course*, in *La Bamba*'s screenplay, Luis Valdez accentuates how the *Living-You*'s familial dramas surface as ixipltas of Quetzalcoatl & Tezcatlipoca: "There's [a] god of culture, Quetzalcoatl, the feathered serpent, [who] . . . surfaces in *La Bamba* as the figure of Ritchie Valens. He's an artist & poet & is gentle & not at all fearful."

Ritchie, *Living-You*, *Movie-You*,
we'd like to introduce you

to *Serpent-You*.

IX.

Dear Ritchie,

I love the scenes in *La Bamba* as you wander through the high school halls with your guitar, your obsession always a desirable weight strapped to your shoulder. Having spent much of my high school days not in class but in a public library far from all the stares & mocking comments, I let myself dream into you. But the spring after Daniel's death—my first undergraduate literature course at a community college—free for recent high school grads & the only school that would take me, being 260 out of 273 in my graduating class—& there, Ritchie, sitting in the back of the classroom, long hair veiling my face, I watched the professor glance around the room, searching, & not knowing his students quite yet, he said he needed to read an essay he'd received for the first paper, &, Ritchie, my muscles tensed, my doe in headlights, a cliché stuck beneath language, as he read my entire essay to the class, calling it a beautiful reading of a poem, that *this* is what he expected from our class, & in the back of the room, my cringe & curl pouting, I refused to look up, scared he'd say my name, pulling everyone's eyes to me.

But on that day, Ritchie, after class, the professor signaled me to wait. Ritchie, he told me, "how wonderful," my close reading of Rilke had been, & I mumbled something, not knowing how to receive a compliment, scurrying off quickly after, & that night, not having tied a noose in months, I decided if I was going to live, if I was going to fulfill my pledge to *Daniel-You*, I'd need space & time to survive my own persecuting eyes—to learn to stand, see, & feel, taste, hear, touch—my heart pulsing as world together.

When I told my parents, my mother's face stoic despite her tears, they nodded, radically compassionate, allowing me the months to undergo what, with what I know now today about dioxins & our family's DNA, I would never choose again. Ritchie, somehow getting accepted as a transfer student to the local university, I deferred enrollment for a semester.

Alone twenty of the twenty-four, I planned—I would play guitar eight hours a day, practicing singing, so I could then apply to the Berklee College of Music, because, well, Ritchie, you know: I wanted to rock, it was always about the music.

Naive? My intuition opens when operating at my most naive. An infancy in a world without claim,

starcoal blurring the char-shores
         soft, the water

as perfect as parachutes
everything spiraling, awe wrought awe.

At that time, I didn't know the terms *neurodiverse*, *Agent Orange*, or *synesthesia*, or how deeply sensitive to all stimuli my flesh is, but music & writing have always been twin consolations to the noise; however, instead of practicing guitar & singing, Ritchie, during my reeducation, I read hundreds of books of poetry & philosophy; my younger brother, always the kindest & most compassionate of us, would go to the library to retrieve the list of books given him by his brooding older brother, because, Ritchie, the first five months of treatment, my skin erupted all over my body, head to toe, ballooning up as the drug refabricated my skin, & the doctor saying, *It is just a* unique *response; we don't know why*, prescribing antidepressants, & midnight staring into the bathroom mirror, I would shake my head, Ritchie, crying quietly, "This isn't me, this isn't me," over & over again, until, how many silent months later, swung scar swung, gripping a promise tight in my hands like some rope bridge swinging over a chasm, *this vow* to a young man whose promise had already drowned in blood that I'd swallowed, which, daily, flowered in me, a thousand petals suddenly crying awake, &, Ritchie, one day, I looked up & saw, not my skin, but the patterns of my days, the recurring designs my thoughts took when "my" was *my*ing—& I laughed, Ritchie, I could only laugh with the spirals, & soon, my self-refusal curled shrimp small knowingly into a stoic but steadfast chum, just one of so many vice-voices, &, Ritchie, soon JOY was where the walls fall, tongue, unyielding abandon-song, singing:

"Break from under the compass,
let the white, the gray, & the casting—

we the graveyard of mammals, *we* ivory the gravestone."

Singing, "*We* my *I* for the dark cries
until only the purple is still."

& here, Ritchie, your kiss silks, every light point brushing each other
against night, sky drowned under all the feathers of all the fallen angels
in the fields where the dying roan bays.

It was beautiful.

We were beautiful.

[YES,]

—We Belong Together

an *Angello Fabrication*

Yes, we'll erect a temple over the noun-heart & tendril, & yes, concrete fact is impossible, an enigma, for this flesh-making exists between seeing, & yes, we grow light like a pair of birds opening beak to feed from beak, & yes, we crawl forward like a caterpillar caressing the hand's rind curve, & yes, solemn is the word that lives, obscurity as blessed, in the dust, our earth, our yes to yes all our pierced disregards.

X.

Dear Ritchie,

Growing older has its perks, but the warped records of my spinal
collection are less MBV & more Merzbow, but at forty-four, we've learned
to love how we love our distortions, the pain needles piercing as quiet
lightning w/o rain, & yes, *Textual-Me* knows *Movie-You* loves this kind of
overdrive, as in *La Bamba*, when you auditioned in the garage, & *Los
Lobos-You* sang out of *Movie-You*'s mouth, & it was all Saturday night on
Tuesday afternoon, like heaven on earth, time collapsing, the sound like
silver resonances refracted, chalice chiming as if each were their own
glittering surfacing endless self-reflections, nearly cliché funhouse-mirror
trope, but there, with you, we weren't scared, no, as one vibration to
another, it was home, a shimmer glide, &, Ritchie, we've agreed, no
matter how scratched our vinyl, as long as I can hear you, I'll keep
tracing shapes in the popcorn ceiling when it's too painful to stand

> (a porcelain milkmaid; a marble-carved St. Francis
> withered beside a gaunt lion; porcelain Siamese
> cats: one smiling, one frowning; glass lamps with
> irises in amber overlay, bats in deep amethyst;
> meadows of grapes, wheat & fruits; dogs & stilted
> unicorns wandering valleys of snow; a peach-blown Cupid
> sharpening his glass arrow against a rotating
> grindstone).

XI.

Ritchie,

This morning my seven-year-old niece told me a story about a girl in her class asking her if she was a "dirty Mexican," & frowning, I recalled a conversation with my mother two days prior, when my mother reminded me: when I was five, when *we* were the only "colored" people in the freshly painted suburban all-American picket fence dream on the northwest side of a pretty square town; my mother said, one day, after playing on the sparkly slide side of the park, I stumbled home, crying, & *Baby-Me* told my *Mom-Then* that an older, tall, freckle-faced, red-haired boy kept calling me a "dirty Mexican," & my mom said I cry-sighed to her, "I take showers, Mommy, I'm not

> dirty,"
> &, Ritchie,
> heart emojis
> > pop-tart

around me as I try to remember being such a small bucktoothed bowl-cut, &, Ritchie, this morning, forty years older than four feet, I asked my niece how *she* replied, & my niece flipped her long, chestnut-brown hair over her shoulder, & after an intentionally dramatic pause, she lifted her chin, & rocking her head on her neck, all Beyoncé-Queen-B-has-deemed-you-*Oh-No-You-Didn't*, she said, "I told her I was a Martinez, & then I pushed her butt to the ground," &, Ritchie, fireworks smiling out of the corner of her eyes, for one moment we were both one anticipation, then, heads thrown back, we're braying trombones, stomping merry—joy our preferred stereotype.

[WE]

—We Belong Together

an *ANGELLO FABRICATION*

We winter in the space between the Minotaur & the unbroken sentence. We sup on entrails of gods foolishly wakened, & there, a boy opens his eye, & follows the trail left by his mother, & there, a grandmother dies only to return in the form of a word. We die into our words &, thereby, lucidly demand a room for the spirit that is the body, for there is not spirit, only body, & we follow its traces through time. We take a quetzal, & tear its feathers from the skin, only so many beasts in our belly. We are pregnant with *this*: a thousand berries jump out from the comma, but there is a limit to that trick, a limit to the rummaging through language to know the other world.

XII.

Dear Ritchie,

Another cyster grows on my hip: smaller than the peach-sized child that nested along my spine that, once removed, left a wide crater hollow mid-back; similar in size to the one removed from my chest, the one just right of my heart, whose scar as softer deep as their absence but larger than the randomly & gully away smoothly rising & falling across all my pore fields, toe to groin, groin to scalp. & I don't miss them, my scalpel born, these that skin-stretched my neck tight as paralysis, in the impossible that, unexpectedly, ruptured a dream where I shared the stage with lyricists whose work I loved, me, *just a kid from Pacoima*, &, Ritchie, Mt. Etna bleeding, I remembered how nervous you were before *Movie-You* got up on stage, & said, *Here's a bit of a rattlesnake*, an iridescent masculinity in rhinestone, & heels, lavender snakeskin blazer shimmering from the heat, &, Ritchie, I'll never be *Movie-You*, fear sometimes slips me on as its skin, a knowing leer beetles wear, spider mites webbing leaf & stem, killing all the roses, but, Ritchie, that night, my doves committed themselves to winglessness, & you took the stage, no paranoia the blood would soak the gauze to stain my collar, but instead, God began the seasons from impossibility, a smile the skin makes from sunrise.

Ritchie, what *you* meant was, I stood, scarrise bright.

divot-tracing   the scar
on the back of your neck
      where the pearl

pressured   for softer skies,
the cyst-hollow you left
  on the neck
      in yourself with the shape

regret takes   as it grows
its bereft valley, a glade
  you left
     the width of a fist,

as if,   mirroring
growth outward, the polyp
  its valley glade
     punched inward,

pushing for   the core horizon
where your setting light pulses
  outward,
     cloudless, skin thrust in

for primordial   collapse;
& you, in tracing you,
  where light pulses
     heartward, softly rocking

beside the windowsill   as the snow
falls outside into the alley
  & you collapse,
     no light escaping,
     against the soft

drift on the oil-   stained lime
dumpster overflowing

outside into
              crushed Coors boxes;

I'm humming like Humpty Dumpty
on his wall before all the king's
    dumpster
              men & all the king's horses

lose against   the shattered
puzzle of his shell, you watch
    all the kings,
              & laugh at the snowflakes,

their will   to escape
singularity by drifting,
    puzzle shell,
              through the violence

for a driftsmore subtle union,
    not a snow's white dress,

but a smile   tossed
with a quick nod & glance
    to disappear
              to a person you don't want

as you pass
    & glance at
        each other outside

the lavatory in one more blank
echoing hall; but now, you,
    with you,
        imagine, there, in the anonymity

of   that passage,
all the king's men

in the glistening   otherside
of his shattered shell,
    at you,
        & this time, instead of passing

their smiles silently, you'll point
darker down the passage, deeper
    past his shattered
        into the nesting mirror

abandoned   in your neck,
& as the knights gallop forth,
    darker down
        through its resonance

    into flesh, you would
    turn for a frown

                turned upside

out &
                slapped back

        together again.

PTSD FAIL OF THE WEEK

Before all our voices
become pixels,

just toilet rolls to be
tossed—tell me it's OK.

I'll never be enough,
seesaw me higher:

your trash can fits
my smile every time

the bear traps me
between my teeth.

XIII.

R., I dreamed of you, but you weren't you, you were A. D. from our undergrad years, &, Ritchie, you drove me through an auburn landscape where peach trees grew like titanic sequoias, thrusting high through clouds into the upper atmosphere, their fruit swinging over the earth like fuzzy moons on which we played guitar among Grecian-like ruins, chords churning riffs as the planet's four suns set in orange & violet hues, &, Ritchie, after I woke to "reality," I reminisced on the freshmen hours we spent studying philosophy, debating metaphysics, nodding our heads in unison over our love of the Smashing Pumpkins, My Bloody Valentine, the Cure, &, Ritchie, I remembered how, one autumn twilight, walking to get sushi, fallen leaves blood-slick on the sidewalk, *A. D.-You* fell hard to the gutter, & instinctively, Ritchie, I raced to lift you, your body so light it was as if your bones were hollow, as if the epilepsy that'd seized & compressed your childhood spine for curve had been human crafting you for a glass flute, &, Ritchie, as I held you, I could feel all your keys & joints, & I thought, you, at twenty-one, weighed less than my infant niece's smile, & as I lifted you to your feet, we stared into each other's sighs, suddenly thrust into our final kiss, Act 3, when *Movie-Us* tears through our inhibitions, our evasions, but looking into your happy eyes, I whispered, *I don't kiss boys with hair longer than mine,* even as your hair reached to my shoulder, because, Ritchie, I was always scared then, & yes, yours was longer, hair reaching down your back, & still, you laughed, your staccato & my shy harmonizing as I helped you find your balance, my Boy Scout brushing the leaf from your dirty-blond hair.

[BELONG]

—We Belong Together

an *Angello Fabrication*

I remember hearing "To Here Knows When" as I crunched through leaves & snow: my skin knew love as a snowflake melted on my cheek—it was this incomprehensible, a soft avalanche of whispers, growing until all the world was rose-tinted static, a singularity refusing time & shape, & this sound itself the commitment beneath all purpose, that which drives the primal elements to resolve into human contour, human reverie.

XIV.

Ritchie,

Did you believe in "spirits"? Nearing the climax of *La Bamba*, when Bob took you to see the curandero, the first time I witnessed that scene, an understanding opened from within my life & energies walked through: my mother & I, hand in hand, crossing a dirt parking lot to see her curandera for my first time.

The apartment smelled of fresh laundry, & tortilla, had *Dad*-tall stacks of laundry arranged haphazardly on the floor; it reminded me of home, Ritchie, of my grandma's kitchen in the colony. Then, Ritchie, there, partly hidden by drying sheets, sitting on a plastic chair, was an older, portly woman. She was a blank flower in a sea of solids.

A fate shuffler, la curandera divined with a deck of tarot cards. She fanned the cards facedown on the small yellow metal table; then, in my memory, the spread of cards is replaced with seven cards, all faceup on the table; then, my memory blurs, & I hear a flurry of Spanish spin between the two women, & the cards are sucked up into that tornado of speech, chance caught in the whirl of words I couldn't understand, & then, Ritchie, we're outside, across the parking lot, & it's dark, I turn to look back, & in the shadows of evening, from behind her door, a light emanates out from all sides.

Ritchie, did *Real-You* believe in fate? &, Ritchie, *Movie-You* was fated the minute you were written. & so fated, how did *Movie-You* understand Bob when he translated the curandero? "He says life is a snake. A snake crawling out of its own dead skin—like a dream."

Life as coiling transformation you ate for breakfast, Ritchie. I don't know, Ritchie, but speaking with love, I think we always seek that place where we are the key point, the choice of choices manifesting. Ritchie, where the sinew, the barbed firing of neurons to the cartilage snapping for prayer or fist, we spire. & here, that bright point, what we name spirit, soul moves *outside story* as *this* singing meat performing faces, all crying Being, Ritchie. We all cry *Be*, Ritchie.

I just think we all forget to live that way sometimes.

If we could only hold there, for across the spectrums of love is this curtain pierced through with all the light that makes all the patterns; dancing, we slide the precipice opening anticipation, the *we* points space-time unfurls as infancy for raw worlding. & there, as this raw *no-you* as awe, Ritchie, you surface.

Ritchie, I scrape the narratives from my skin, for there is no beginning, middle, or end; outside time, ear into the soft, it is *this* emptiness I want: our sacred outside existing only in each other.

[TOGETHER]

—We Belong Together

an *ANGELLO FABRICATION*

Being, one & changeless, but enfleshed, existents ever agitating between all the properties of love, the very substance within all the forms, a vapor palacing the heart concealed in our speech, corresponding to the forms of our knowledge, reality tasting like our sweat-dewed skin after you bit my lip bloody, your cum salty on my pink.

XV.

Ritchie,

Have you ever heard of ixiptlas? I think *Movie-You*'d recognize them. *Movie-You* might've seen them in Tijuana, around LA, in your house. I grew up around them, at my grandma's, in my curandera's home, even at the Catholic church I attended as a child. They were, in Nahua culture, sculptures, visions, drawings, paper cuttings, humans, all depictions of energies ("gods") that *were* the "gods," some destined for sacrifice.

Ritchie, *Ritchie* as ixiptla.

Critic & artist Mariana Castillo Deball states, "Without having to visually appear the same, multiple ixiptlas of the same god could exist simultaneously. The distinction between essence & material, & between original & copy vanishes."

Translations of *ixiptla* render poorly when crossing the colonial abyss: the term's potential closes, at best, into mere mimetic personification. These comprehensions of ixiptlas are, to me, lacking. Ixiptlas rise, focused, localized energies emerging & receding, in motion, not static imitations mimicking static "presence." Ixiptlas, as so understood, were part of an epistemic/ontocorporal world that seems experientially of an order outside an aesthetics of mimesis. (That is, if we see the history of poetics, let alone "poetry" itself as a colonial object—maybe this is why poetry, let alone art, for the last century, has been episodically declared dead; Eva Geulen has written, "As a discourse, the end of art is one of our modern traditions.") Perhaps *that* tradition unveils itself as a colonial object? The way our stories tell us before we learn to tell them & how we were molded.

It seems so much of 20th-century English poetics, its very conception, emerges activated from an epistemic poverty (perhaps intentional, perhaps unintentional), an aesthetic epistemicide, one excluding the varied & dynamic knowledges of the indigenous, the colonized, the oppressed, knowledges that, sociologist Boaventura de Sousa Santos states, "are the unsaids of those unsaids . . . unsaids that emerge from the abyssal line dividing metropolitan & colonial societies & sociabilities in Western-centric modernity." Here, in the colonizing aesthetic governing the image, mimetic theory cleaves *how* one *knows* & *undergoes* "the thing," its lives traumatized, as if the "one" cannot also be plural, & the same.

XVI.

&, Ritchie, how *they* hunger-spout with such wounded entitlement, but
this time, I have to tell you, counterprotesters played *La Bamba* over
white $upremacists holding a rally in Shelbyville, Tennessee. I think
you'd be proud, the sound drowning out the terrorism.

> But, Ritchie, I hear *this entitlement*
> when *Movie-Bob*, as he's scripted,
>
> confesses to raping *Movie-Rosie*,
> just before *Movie-You* punches him
>
> away, saying, "I'm not Rosie."
> This never *really* happened.
>
> It is invention. For drama. Written
> for the cinematic violence
>
> of the sacrificed feminine
> troped to the bed.
>
> But if this were "true," Ritchie,
> what would *Real-You* have done?
>
> No forgiveness for rapist *Movie-Bob*,
> would you still follow the script & do nothing?
>
> Yes, my mom did everything she could for
> her three sons, similar to your troped
>
> *Movie-Mom*, Ritchie, but my mother was matriarch
> with a list of demands, leather belts, & vacuum cords,
>
> a perfectionist whose pacifist husband laid
> disciplinary duties in her less than passive hands.

My father, celebrating July 4th, burned down his father's corn fields
with a stray firework when I was in fifth grade? Who was your father
figure, Ritchie? Whose patriotism forms a father? What would your
father figure about the movie's sexualities across the spectrum?

Ritchie, it's always *Movie-Bob*, crossing a line,

straddling the Harley, revving to ride,
the leather embodiment of desires,

& there's that incestuous tender
scene of *Esai Morales-Bob*

sliding into bed with *Lou Diamond-Ritchie*,
& yes, we all know *they* aren't "real"
brothers, & this doesn't seem like

it's the first time *Esai Morales-Bob*
has commented on *Diamond-Ritchie's*

ass, some kind of fan-
based shipping, ready-

made for *La Bamba* rock opera,
& here, Bob, his drunk violence

turned against desire's margins, when he seemingly laughs at the possible
"shock" to sensibility he might provoke, it doesn't seem aimed at *Movie-
You*, Ritchie, his laugh seems aimed at us, the movie's audience; as if *Esai
Morales-Bob* knows he isn't *Real-Bob*, & *Lou Diamond-Ritchie* knows he's
not *Real-You*, & both aren't ashamed of how they fantasize, & what they
choose to do, they both know boundaries are watched to be made, & they
spectrum more freely; but then,

what would *Elizabeth Peña-Rosie* think?

Or maybe, *Esai Morales-Bob* knows Valdez wrote you as
Quetzalcoatl, & he, opposite, as Tezcatlipoca, the night sky,
discord, rulership, hostility, & conflict, & *Esai Morales-Bob* knows

pantomimed love makes excess ethical for tonal boundaries, & this is his part of the spectrum to play:

Movie-Bob as *Esai Morales-Bob* as agonistic love;

& maybe this explains why *Movie-Bob* is the only character to develop, suddenly a sober sensible father cradling his daughter, while you, Ritchie, *Movie-You*, don't take this the wrong way, well, you're kind of overdriven static. Cinematic ascension pulsing. Unforgettable trauma octaves.

You're cinematic surfacing of transhistorical aesthetic impulses shocking erotic political rock ballads out of the mouth of an adolescent's fever dream of freedom. What I mean is, I think you're cool.

XVII.

Ritchie,

There's such hunger for the messianic; it is a dangerous drug: to desire *one who answers all*—to follow that yellow brick road where the "wizard" resides (worse if you *want to be the one & only* "wizard"). Such hocus pocus.

Utopia . . . always either too far gone or yet to be.

Past, present, future. How profound, how potent these one- to two-syllable words are as they pin our bodies to singular "selves."

I hear, pinned wings struggling, Walter Benjamin's "Angel of History."

His face is turned toward the past. Where we perceive a chain of events, he sees one single catastrophe which keeps piling wreckage upon wreckage & hurls it in front of his feet. The angel would like to stay, awaken the dead, & make whole what has been smashed. But a storm is blowing from Paradise; it has got caught in his wings with such violence that the angel can no longer close them. The storm irresistibly propels him into the future to which his back is turned, while the pile of debris before him grows skyward. This storm is what we call progress.

Do Angels have a concept for gender, Ritchie? A "he" of wings battered by stormy winds? Here, I prefer Rilke's Angels, outside the binary, spectral energies of flesh-born, yet earthless, feather.

Speaking of Angels, Ritchie, yesterday I was reading Angel Dominguez's elegant prism, "A Backyard Funeral Afterparty para Latinidad." In this gorgeous essay reflecting on particle physics, the surfacing of the many faces of what has come to be called "Latinidad," Angel writes,

"We cannot deify any ancestor, advocate, scholar, thinker, writer, etc., as each is human & ultimately riddled with human error."

Angel Dominguez's essay navigates the messy history of the racializing noun, Ritchie, & of that desire for the messianic. It would be impossible to sum up an essay rooted in diffusion, or, as Angel writes, "Perhaps this essay itself is another moment of decoherence."

As one whose "neurodiversity," whose "disabilities," apparently, surface from chemical "decoherence," I resonate with this essay's wavelength: these identifying racialized terms are political emergencies, not ontologies; when these "names" surface, they demarcate a positionality never static; it is a graceful essay critiquing the colonial project & its demands for essentiality.

Essentially, we're each having a particle experience in this vast field of "Latinidad," & some of the particles are demanding that we all assimilate into the same particle positioning, insisting that it is not representative of the particle but in fact, the field as a whole. Yet the field itself suggests that all possible positions of the particle are not only possible but in fact happening in their own individual worlds.

Ritchie, here is an Angel whose humility toward the flow is acceptance of the flesh as a plural being: we flash only briefly as a multicellular ark, one whose conception of consciousness must evolve beyond *one* time & *one* history; Ritchie, we must shed that skin. Let them pathos & pathologize, we're no one's noun.

Ritchie, I love singing "La Bamba," "Yo no soy marinero, soy capitán," but as *my* Angel of History has written, there ain't no/know captain, merely the ocean whose water it is temporarily composed of—we ship as the ship whose form is a water momentarily frozen into form—we the vessel that is itself the medium, as what we perceive as "all" is only the moment of our own humility come to consciousness, & the darkness beyond already spreads within like a honey for which we are the wax.

Holographic, Ritchie, you surface everywhere & nowhere, each & none nonlocal emergencies, winged guitars, not against time, but constituting itself in dispersing itself as *world*, diffused across, & between these horizons of commodified distraction.

> Ritchie, partake of the honeycomb
> & flare, a star imploding
> to swallow & hold
>
> all the unseen worlds.
>
> That said, Ritchie, I'm embarrassed to ask,
>
> but do you think we could
>
> get together sometime
>
> & decolonize?

[TOGETHER]

—We Belong Together

an *ANGELLO FABRICATION*

We are a thousand measures of a life bound together: a bracelet, a locket of human hair, the fever spread from solace to solace after the light has lay dead to rise again from beneath human breath, thus, the measure of intimacy in memory, the distance the body travels to know another: propolis & juniper, sap latent within leaf to the bark. The juncture where moss climbs.

XVIII.

Ritchie,

As *Movie-You* stood onstage,
as *Lou Diamond-You* lip-synched

"La Bamba," did *Living-You* feel
its transnational aesthetic

surfacing through as
a spectral body of "color quebrado"

as your tongue as
son jarocho Afro-Mexican traditions?

As you translated the verses
from the Spanish you didn't speak,

did *Living-You* hear an aural
emission of multiple temporalities

& "broken colors"?
I'd like to think you did, Ritchie.

I'm writing you as if you're everything
that will answer, but really, Ritchie,

there's only you & this page.
Just like there's only me writing this.

Even if you didn't know,
was it all for rock & roll

appropriation, Ritchie?
Or has it always been rebellion?

Ritchie, who knows
what a lyric is, or should do

this side of the epistemicide?
I don't know, Ritchie.

You might've
gotten Twitter-

canceled today, Ritchie,
still, I love how *Movie-You*

was *David Hidalgo-Voice-You*
when the movie premiered

in 1987, & today, you've got 40,827,394 views
on fake JustinBieber's "official" YouTube;

with love, I follow a lover's compass,
& with love, return me, Ritchie,

to our mangrove world
oriented outside time-

territories to rule over us,
Ritchie, let's glide-guitar-ta

with eye-shadow wings,
like Boaventura de Sousa Santos,

"Reality cannot be reduced to what exists

because what exists is only the visible
part of reality that modern absyssal

thinking defines as being
on this side of the line & within

whose confines it elaborates its theories."

Metonymically speaking,
Ritchie, I gotta confess:

border spectrums
that spectrum
the no-sound,

I have no idea who the fuck "you" "are,"
let alone who the fuck "I" "am,"

but perhapsly,
with faith-whistles,
we'll valentine

      each
      other
      again

pinkly dustfuzzing
caterpillar whiskers,

just us shimmer
sigh-loudlies.

XIX.

Ritchie,

Was music a kind of drag for you? In 1958, when your producer, Bob
Keane, sliced your name in half from *Valenzuela* to *Valens*, was he keen to
the violence performed (historical, epistemic, psychological, etc.) to sell
you?

Did you feel more acceptable to white listening?

Could they hear the absent -*zuela*
in the tremolo of your voice?

Were you Donna's zuela? Too brown
to be attractive? But as *Ritchie Valens*,
a name all radio race transcendent,
when she heard you, was she finally
attracted *to you* as you sang *her* name?

Ritchie, does prettiness equate with
pettiness?

Zuela, possibly meaning "small,"
"little," or a despective, "always
looked down upon."
Zuela, also an adze, a cutting tool, as
if Keane wielded your own name
against itself.
Zuela, according to Urban Dictio-
nary: "A loyal guy friend who no one
wants to get with because, despite
their loyalty, they are wholly un-
attractive."

Poetry was my petti-dress. All zuela in adolescence, unaware my father's
genetics had been manipulated before my birth, his wartime exposure to
Agent Orange, that, when I discovered *this language*, I found facelessness.
No mouth, all word. & I wanted to be pretty, so I powdered my face with
verbs, wore my nouns like disposable nylons, learned to sew line breaks to
my tongue, so, when I wrote, no one could hear my skin bleeding. At
home, I practiced walking the runway heeled, hips swaying & swinging.

Ritchie, I didn't want to be ugly. I wanted to be *Michael*. But sometimes,
words are so loud you can't see yourself. You start hallucinating in blond
& blue eyes.

Ever the contrarian, I preferred Front 242, nylons, & powdering my face smooth.

Ironically, Ritchie, now, when my closest friends edit my poetry, those who know my linguistic tricks & gambles, they write "T.P." (*Too Pretty*) to mark what should be cut, something "trivial" that doesn't "add" to the poetic.

But what if we don't "add up" this time, Ritchie? What if this time, we dress ourselves in our own insignificance, all blood, pus, & skirts. I want to hear it all, Ritchie, the little & the big. Let's put a band together where our tongue & skin sound the most gorgeous distortion, a sonic shitstain sonneting in rhinestone & rouge. Let's write poetry, all T.P., & no flush. We'll be a zuela dancing faceless, two Chicanx cupcakes in Donna drag, listening outside white & black.

[FOR]

—We Belong Together

an *ANGELLO FABRICATION*

To hollow our beauties for a child walking, having just learned for another, bounding forth in the freedom of maneuver & evade for the trees wrapped in Christmas lights like limbs knotted in twine for the leaves pale gray, leather strips hanging from their stem for the sound of strollers edging forth, for the turn of an unborn baby brain emerging into its first sound for a child's play, the sounds, the drop of a football & the high voice of a little boy wearing sunglasses for he trips over intentions for his waiter, delivering sushi, tall & muscular.

XX.

The liberation, or authentication, of all voices in poetry in society leads to madness. Toward this the lyric tends.

      —Allen Grossman, *The Sighted Singer*

Dear Ritchie,

I know you'll never read this, but sometimes a letter doesn't need to be read, it just needs to be written, & I've written your every song to allow me to fall outward until only my wings are left. Icarus I am not. I was the wax wilting behind the feather. I was the frameless between the star & ocean. Ritchie, I am left only scars to silt to sing to sew only my seizure to your sorrows.

I've run out of methods to be "normal." Ritchie, I'm tired. Of surviving their "understanding." They once said "mentally handicapped," now they say "neurodiverse," they once said "attention deficit with hyperactivity," now they say "autism spectrum disorder," &, Ritchie, I tell you I *hear* all the colors; they said "cripple," now they say "physically disabled," I tell you my spine has always curved as a harp, nerve plucked gold, while my skin opened a thousand mouths in chorus, pigment draining, cyst-sung, no border between exterior & interior, this membrane not the sole game between citizenship & consciousness.

A report on Agent Orange published by the National Birth Defect Registry in 2017 states:

Dioxin appears to act like a persistent synthetic hormone interfering with important physiological signaling systems that can lead to altered cell development, differentiation & regulation.

Ritchie, Agent Orange is nearly synonymous with dioxins; the report details the differences "in functional & structural deficits" between children of Vietnam veterans & the children of nonveterans. The report states that there is no way to tell, right now, how long this "*persistent synthetic hormone*" continues altering one's cells.

From my father to me, & Ritchie, I don't have children but my brothers do: my now eighteen-year-old niece's scoliosis, a telltale expression of dioxin's work, was so severe, nearly 45 degrees, she opted to fuse her spine (like *A.D.-You*, Ritchie, as I'll do in time).

She gave me permission to tell you Ritchie.

Ritchie, of the tumors, the allergies, the neurological differences, the violences, the supposed learning "disabilities," the skin "disorders," the emotional/behavioral differences, & the thirty-eight "Miscellaneous Defects" the report details, which, Ritchie, I'm afraid to say, sixteen I navigate daily, what is this, Ritchie?

My niece said I was brave to write you what I've just learned—that this isn't just "neurodiversity," or "disability."

This is patriotism Ritchie.

◆

       Porous the boundaries between borders
       Porous the skin
       Porous the skin borders
       between a father & son

Of his time as military police at the Phan Rang Air Base, of the first time my father spoke to me of his service in Vietnam, this gentle, kind man, this humble & quiet man confessed shooting men caught strung in barbwire; it was the morning after I held *Daniel-You* gunshot in my arms, my lips reddened; I stood there, quiet as my father fell to his knees in tears, saying, "I know what it's like; I want to forget . . . "

       Porous a collapse decorated in swords
       Porous the strife by which we love
       Porous my heart, my father, my Ritchie

& Ritchie, my birthday, March 29, was officially named Vietnam Veterans Memorial Day by *that* 45th. Tomorrow, I'll memorialize my father, but I can't forget, a year ago, Adam Toledo, a thirteen-year-old "special education" student, though empty handed, though child arms raised, was killed by Chicago Police Department officer Eric Stillman.

Porous the frontier between birth & death
Porous the ocean's deepest sapphire
Porous the becoming world

Porous, we ask why we are alive again
when the black curls
beneath the kiss—

Porous the threshing tongue
Porous unyielding abandon-song.

WHAT MY FATHER SOUGHT ABOVE ALL

A father's harvest. The apricot bruise. Sunset across every wing. On Fourth of July. We skies of fireworks. Erupting white sparkles against. Wheat ash. All the burned feathers. In such Christlight. Your eyes stained. Glass-sung. His childhood farm. We all are. All womb wide. Every acre innocent. Clawed. Back into our arms. Cornfields to wander. Each word.

> The moregift. Opening.
> Through the night.

> Where only you & I remain—
> sparkling against

> such dark portraits.
> All my infant carving out the old.

Because we were never exiles. Only lighthouses.

[ETERNITY]

—We Belong Together

an *ANGELLO FABRICATION*

Fold with time into multiples of mind melt leaving a sorrow as wide as love. Could we uncouple "the past" from its fold with the "present"? Like worms made one into two with a slice, how does a meteor cause crashing waves? Instead, let us pass echoes to each other—the world is no further than this: our shared space turned fig upon the palm, our we-wing wasp wending inside, feeding off such lush gardens unpeeled to human eyes, so many skyless dreams ravenous beneath our childhoods.

XXI.

Ritchie,

I wonder if you'd like Hölderlin. He wrote, "Everything that *is* interpenetrates as soon as it becomes active." Don't you love that?

Empedocles wrote, "All things unite in one through love."

Sometimes, Ritchie, *Donna* emanates from everything, everywhere. *Love*, not simply a sentimental feeling or an ethical imperative. A cosmic force. Ritchie, for both Hölderlin & Empedocles, the forces of *Love & Strife* materially (re)organizes creation. Moreover, these cosmic forces, fashioning & ordering "trees & men & women, beasts & birds & water-bred fishes, & the long-lived gods too," also inhabit & order the individual lives of humanity.

　　　　They are in us, Ritchie; they are us, Ritchie.

Maybe, when the curandero gave you the necklace, he was trying to balance your *love* with your *strife?* Maybe, he was trying to rewrite the script &, through death, wake you to life?

Maybe I'm just dreaming. Friedrich Hölderlin dreamt of Empedocles. Hölderlin wrote, "Empedocles is a son of the heavens . . . a human being in whom those opposites are united so intensely that they become one in him, divesting themselves of their original distinguishing form & thus reversing themselves."

　　　　　　　You're my Empedocles, Ritchie.
　　　　　　　Just like you're my Donna,
　　　　　　　My ixiptla Orpheus on the spectrum
　　　　　　　　　　descending.
　　　　　　　To turn & lose yourself. Higher.

◆

Ritchie, a pure life, according to Hölderlin, is attained when the oppositional *natural/aesthetic* reconcile & divest themselves of themselves in each other. There, between, surfaces the divine.

Movie-You as *Real-You* as *Text-You* as *German-You* as *Pre-Socratic-You* as *Donna-You* as *Daniel-You.*

In the myth, Empedocles committed suicide, throwing himself into a volcano, Mt. Etna in Sicily. Ritchie, *Movie-You* & *Real-You* die in a plane crash. Driven forward, guitar in hand, to reconcile your waking life with *La Bamba*'s opening dream of death, Ritchie, you sing, you & your music "a more mature, true, purely universal intensity."

FORTY-FOUR

It's September XX of 2022, Ritchie.

I've been alive for 1,403,970,293,432 milliseconds,

yet for all my unfashioned architectures,

Ritchie, I'm so many beautiful puppets:

apparently, Aries to the marrow,

but, Ritchie, stars & fates caught in capital,

let's promise to trade decolonized tarot cards

later? I pillow-cuddled your sheet shape

last night, as if it were you, your lavender coconut-oil

lotion you smooth over your cheekbones,

& around your eyes, &, Ritchie, the morning sings—

can you hear, blurring, reverb tidal pink,

the orgasm, yesterday, our sunset shared with us?

III

Ritchie Valens: I'm gonna be a star. . . .
because stars don't fall out of the sky, do they?
      —Luis Valdez, *La Bamba*

Partaking of the dyad, six represents matter and existence that are eternal
but not immutable, since everything divisible is mutable and material.
      —Marianne Shapiro, *Hieroglyph of Time: The Petrarchan Sestina*

Little triumph with a mirror, breath, or handprint . . . humble habitats
of ghosted flesh as on the threshold of speech. . . .
viscous secretions, as well voluptuous.
      —Roberto Tejada, *Still Nowhere in an Empty Vastness*

MY LSD ORPHEUS

to Ritchie Valens, *May 13, 1941–February 3, 1959*

i.

R.,
you

sow
praise

seer
seized:

seas,
air

seared:
you

praise
so

sewn.
See,

prey

errs,

ewe

cered.

Sere-
sown,
you

seed

heirs,

pries

praise

sears,

ere

so

seized,

                              you
                              yew;
                    praise
          ceased,
                    seer,

                              sew
                              air.

ii.

                         R., no
                              grief rose
                              crown rapt,
               no dews
               curved course
                              lasts o'er

               the ore
                              flesh knows
                              as corse;
               necrose
               sundew,
                              berapt,

          in rapped
                         rancor,
               credos
                         foreknown.
          Leprose,

                                             our cores

     in coarse
                                        skin, wrapped
     porose,
     passed o'er

                                        for no
                                        love do:

                         subdued,

            we course
                              misknown,

       overapt
                              pallor

       hell-rose.

       Taurus,
                              life's dew

clamors,
recourse
          spill-rapt

                    spine noun'd.

iii.

       R.,   whose call,
               mouth raw, tongue-
               scarred, led you

                              past our vain

               pleas? Who metes

                              the vast through
                              your mute lips?

                              We whose lips

               mask the col,

                              the lack, through

               which the tongs

                              even death met,

               yanks our veins

                              crook'd, voice hew'd,

               God's own   hue,

                                    those bright lips,
                                    brawl in vain,

               ceaseless calms   pun, meted

                    in throes

                    truths thrall thrown,

       Ritchie, you

                              know we, meat-
made, earthslips
                              flesh molt, caul
love close, vein's

                              pale vervain
coursing through
with folds cull-

                              sharp, hope-hewn,
our corse lips

                              a pallid myt

for those, meeting
no's song, veins

                              like soft lisps
                              singing through,
                              outside hues
Gods may call.

iv.

                              All that we sense
what we see, hoard,
where we meddle
                    salvage & tease,
                    Ritchie, we wield
              imperial right

                                        as if to write
                    were the sole sense
                                        to grasp the weald;
how we've sold, whored
sore our mettle:
                    now, we drink tea

                                        as if all is
lost were our rites

                                        ancient, metal
                                        altars we censed
with laws hoared;

Ritchie, I wheeled

flowers for wealed
lovers teasing

                mislaid hopes; hordes,
of woe, what right

                what hope, what sense
                leads us to mettle

with lost medals?
Paradise wields

                us, we but scents
                it diffused, 'tis,

Ritchie, your song

                stole all dawn's horde

what you sang: hoard,

            now, summer's nettle,
sing our death's rites

            round our meat's weald,
bless it whole: tease

            hell, Eden's sense.

v.

Incarnation cast

            out from the ceaseless
            only names endure,

Christ-mirror riven

            of crib, Ritchie, songs
       in hand, if, again,
       you were to, again,

            run fame's fickle cast,

fall for a love whose songs
were of lips less seized
            by lack—more riven

by what flesh endures:

decay, the ordure
all must wade, again,
& again, we riven

rehearsals, lives cast
in rivers of ceaseless

churn; & our unsung
echoes sound the song
before our lips, inured
with the grave's ceaseless

hunger, by, again,
Cain's envy cast
for Abel's unriven
gift, & love's revenge
spills more rot than song,
more maggots recast
as crown: of what urn-seed
garden would, again,
you sing? R., ceaseless

hope seizes the ceaseless
in callous hands riven
with remove, & again—
outside flesh—the song.
R., enflesh what endures:
love's trunk gnarled—casteless.

vi.

Ritchie, flood creation's lyres
through the heart's pulsing fane,
instruments of idols,
our blood soothes divine burrs
smooth;   eternities pour
through our flesh: we must read

for such flesh   offers rede
fore we fold   into liers

shelled in wood,   shelled in poor
words we would gladly fain
as if Eden's idyll
mirrored death's breathless bier

my love, you bruise, your burr
                    sounds our holiest reed:
this skin flayed of idols,
                                        you raise your lips as
                    lyres
our kiss the only fane,
                                        heaven's chalice—these
                    pores

          opened to bloom & pour
          our corruptions for biers,
          refusing all we feigned,
          our inmost curved for reed
          those sounds all we liars
          deny, our denial's idle

folded outside idols
                                        & false prophecy; poor,
          we endure gods, liars
          promising reprieve,
          burrs
                                                            pulled
                                        free, but our
                                        meat's rede,

          pain, wound—
          our only fane

          we must endure,
          to feign
                              otherwise, such idle
          dream   numbs
dumb dream's reed,
                    to suffer summer's pour,
                                        solar
                              wind, solar bier,
          for flesh wakes flesh, raw lyre.

vii.

For what white am I chartered?
From what seraph's rime-graved wings
do these storms blind our sole sky?
Ritchie, through the glass, what sight,
what wilderness outside grasped
your blameless flask, & did your

joys reach back, your hands, lips, your
spring's iris, that red-ratchet
swung skyward, seed sun grasping
like Icarus, but your wings—
not wax-bound: a song siting,
between womb & faintest sky,

blurs wild, the love wrung of sky,
ichorless angels freed, where your
Gods have flung their cursed, fixed sight
past their own harmony's chartered
law, thrown their burden, winging
the seamless edges, the pargings

shielding our world's grasp
from the astonished null-sky
within all plants, birds—those wings
shadow-shaped by your hands, your
song vying beyond chartered
intensities, where no-sight

radiates, nature citing
hues obscure, eyes heart-gasping
the burning shades, altar'd sky
the praising bell, the ache terra
sounds as parallel smiles swing,
striking flesh, hope's pitch & yaw

turned in, flesh closed; riper, your
thriven, roots grown across sights
partial miracle, past wings,

awe; music now
quivering, the
you,

of pure grasping,
wind's charter:
annunciation's sky.

THE DONNA SONNETS

Infected Text

Donna, where can you be? / Where can you be?
　　　—Ritchie Valens, "Donna"

"Sheltering is a luxury," said Dr. Kirsten Bibbins-Domingo,
the vice dean for population health and health equity at the
University of California, San Francisco School of Medicine.
"In wealthier parts of town, people sheltered earlier and longer,
because it takes resources. Not every community has the
luxury to do that."
　　　　　—Shawn Hubler, Thomas Fuller, Anjali Singhvi, and
　　　　　　Juliette Love, "Many Latinos Couldn't Stay Home.
　　　　　　Now Virus Cases Are Soaring in Their Communities,"
　　　　　　The New York Times, June 26, 2020

COVID-19 continues to disproportionately impact communities of color everywhere. For so many months, the virus was all I thought about. It infected my thoughts in my fear for my friends & family, my loved ones. The unknown as uncontrollable. These sonnets were born of that breathless anxiety. During the first pandemic summer, I practiced a formal escapism: I wrote a sonnet & a sestina a day for two months. This, in hindsight, may have been just one unconscious method I used to exert an invented control over the uncontrollable. As the pandemic continued, Trumpian jingoistic rhetoric ran rampant, voices of white nationalist rhetoric infecting public discourse; and, then, the murder of Ahmaud Arbery, George Floyd, Breonna Taylor, Daunte Wright, . . . & so many others killed by the police . . . yet, for all the horror, the beautiful rise of Black Lives Matter, & the emergence of that summer's protests.

As the summer rolled on, my "love" sonnets themselves were infected: for each sonnet, I rendered an "infected" translation, combining the language from a sonnet with an equivalent number of words, selected by bibliomancy, from white supremacist Greg Johnson's *The White Nationalist Manifesto* (the *WNM*).

Employing a similar process as Tom Mirovski's brilliant prompt "How to Make a Nature Poem," these translations began by distributing DNA codons to represent each word for each individual sonnet, & the language selections from the *WNM*; after, each sonnet had its own unique dictionary of sixty-four DNA codons, each codon representing a potential (set of) word(s) from the collected pool of language from both sonnet & the *WNM*.

From the National Center for Biotechnology Information, I retrieved the DNA sequence of COVID-19's infectious crown, its namesake "corona."

Appearing as gray text, each *infected* sonnet, using its individual codon dictionary, has been rearranged—that is, translated—according to COVID-19's DNA sequence. Text infected.

　　　　Voice, our love models

The scars stage the dragged slights, lies fore splayed,
　　　　the bruise-scarred vales
blind's bride, swoon seize our urn-depths, lips wax light:
　　　　love sworn fore pure struggle:
bruise wake our rose unflayed, & sing, "Days take
　　　　we crave grave's power;
twine, true verdure purls, verve roots swerve blush sighs,
　　　　love, rise soft & struggle

　　　　though community tired wide.
when wise into wild flesh moans more wide."
　　　　White purls, lips splayed, shaped
Love, love shapes our tired soils, vales, & voids,
　　　　crone, now, useless unflayed,
oceans & vast heavens, but fate's white
　　　　metapolitical riper,
sings flesh for birth to root inside grave's voice,
　　　　our fate's White Nationalism 1.0 shapes skin
white sight sings skin sundered sworn for word; voice,
　　　　matter, tears inside useless

　　　　sliced light: white purls, lips
the scalpel's flawed flight: sliced sight for shaped light.

　　　　splayed, wide tongue-swollen
Crave me thornbird, love crone sung, help me hoist

　　　　useless libertarianism bride,
pure concussion, our love's tongue-swollen rites,

　　　　moan our love-sung slights,

　　　　hoist useless sliced voice
our scarred rinds, riper past us; wings rawed thin,

　　　　—white word—true scar approaches.
sound our flowers, spear your tears to my skin.

ii.

Oh, Donna, where *ever always* throws lots

across our foreheads in ash, tame me, name
        Define, oh facing fires,
me to be gatherer, for no love clots
        where name throws
my mouth where loss will not enter, no shape
        risk fruitless—all remains brevity.

        Summer enter rounder land:
erases my name from brevity; place
        me recognizing my political
your bruise, fruitless rounds through fruitless centers,
        rounds for skyward surrender;
under my bruises' surrender; watch, wait
        my for holy,
for what summer remains in death, enter
        my for our lion's other urgency,

        my enter—risk our will's
my trespass here: for honey, engender
        slain-shrine, where youth's shape
the land buried in the lion's tooth, the sapphire

slain-shrine, the skyward risk where death tenders
        waits my enter, urgency natures

us into more open shape, youth's blind fires
        where holy, the absolute political

        just threatened absolute extinction,
reared for rounder ardor, meat crowned holy,
        our moral bruises mouth genocide.
the skyward in hunger sung as flesh godly.

iii.

Neon theft through
Of skin pushing curl & mouth, we worship
society's flesh, our *between*
cascades through our glazed bodies; we, warm plush
below, all glazed slack,
in lavender flume escapes our taut lips
Donna, reign ever graveward
below; like the fluorescent coral brushed,
pluralistic neighbors plural

skin slurred for a flesh sound;
our skin purls the water, slurred sky a lush
The *real* communed, milk
blur made velvet, we sloth ever in verge,
Cain, wreck—love's reign;
& summers stream between our merging touch,
sound your dawn tactics,
drown our body's distinct—a kiss submerged
we'll commune distinct—

plush murder mouth,
in blue: such bruise communed, speaks no sweet words,
murder-Donna, we'll sweet
only neon forget-me-nots; Donna,
you a neon-black curl kiss;
I kiss to drown, I sing to sound, graveward,
praise murder, Donna,
as black milk breaks day to praise slack dawn, the
drown my forget-me-nots,

eve our words profane; like Cain, we rack real
pluralistic.
our flesh for wreck—love's reign ripens death's spill.

iv.

            Sum, races, even text,
Dandelion's soul soft cotton songs swarm & stir
            were against white
just as skies quiet their mouths round before storm;
            races, even text,
Donna, in parallel folds, before birth,
            touch against Eve;
after death, you bear the *yet*, your chest torn
            Eve, non-white

            in book form,
for halo's void; for bloom, you twin our form,

your song, our roots—your touch, truth—as calyx,
            Donna thrones
in world, chapel in sepal, your book is born—
            you tongueless;
at each moment, in all currents, apex.
            savage whites,

            now, savage bloomed,
Devised against perfect sum, of no sex
            demographics non-white
distinct, Ritchie—I dress you as Eve, my Donna:
            sex immigrants;
are words less than thirst, more tongueless than text,
            no more-world, no more fertile.
as seed—both world & want—we, flora,
            Sepal—we, twin Ritchie—

            I to white chapel the book tongueless
savage gardens, root rich in ravage loam,
            if demographic gardens
for radiance between screams, we raw thrones.
            scream against perfect sum.

v.

The alley past the waste bins, graffiti
        Extinction, invasion,
rainbows decree, we're kings, crowned in stain, &
        for our caged void-pearl
Styrofoam—selves pacing, head unsteady,
        these virtues they aisle
my want voices echo *noose sweet*, demand
        causing shoe caged sorry,

        "produce" dismantled fertility.
I tar myself for promise-feathers &

sing, I'll not *not* be *sorry, I'm sorry,*
        All white all blue murder
I'll not *not* fuck up, virtue cuss-caught in
        because white murder
these ten thousand *say-sos*, caged crows—jury—
        immigration policies suffer

        hope's predation—unsafe slain cause
& shoe scuffed, skin blotched, Donna, I scurry

down the dollar store's "produce" aisle, in coarse
        their white down feral,
cotton tops & blue jeans, thumbing curry,
        all suffer whites feral fast.
cans of corn, cans of beans, hunger the source:

craving, we, the void-pearl, the voice plural,

have no windows, our slain hopes debt feral.

vi.

Flying guitar, what we know is you flew
       Inner nails, inherit you
our unseen borders of hunger redrawn,
       Double nails, include you
Donna, among the corn, lettuce, how you
       Inner wages, integrate you
believed rock & roll could spread wider dawns

       Fear economic & white-bred
in wing with the dove to where the frown fawned

the shame shapes hope into mirrors years deep,
       earth, our fear struggles
where we hang by our nails, fingers torn, gnawed;
       under mirrors parting celibacy
we worship such struggles, we wasp & seed,
       these drivings driver gnawed;

       no control songs,
wingless larvae crawling, we tear & bleed
       our arbor roost force
the inner arbor dry, wings parting flesh,
       we control these most anti-natalism,
bitter fear blister bred, songs bittersweet;
       we control these most
what holy survives what we fissure-bless?
       expected bittersweet,

       our fear heritable,
Is love so cleft, Donna? Our wounds garden?
       our fear reproductive.
Heart rent for wings? Paradise roost trodden?

vii.

Mediator, take possession of this

height: of death—there is no place we are not

already passage, knock bruised lip, lost kiss,
   Must traits wasp?
we thresh & hold altar where we have fought,
   Must traits inherit wasp kiss

   & borders ravaged?
self-contesting, self-forsaken, we brought
   Ethnic sound,
inner forces, inner sights, orchids, life,
   we within death's divide,
all the broken, ravaged, all we forgot
   redrawn, wrought & cleansing
to you, the swollen light—through you, swept pride,
   through white impulse;

   people's white spite,
enchained the wasp, its barb we raised as bride,
   yet our grave-birth
to it we wed what rage remains ablaze
   lips after swept light.
after summer's pyre pries death's divide.

Donna, we sought, in sound, for grace a grave,

a sky between tongue & tooth, lips & thirst,

we wrought this crown of fraught of you—for birth.

viii.

& under the thunder, ascension wept:

here, we walk hand in hand, our listless gait
       Walk fractured, you silence,
beneath the sleet's stained silence, the snows kept
       you greed; our hope here,
him here, in the afterword, childhood graved
       song washed white,

       song that enslaved sudden hope
beneath, where you parted his hair; hope braved
       by unfolding summer's hand
us, we, the scythe love lost against itself,
       through extinction;
we, the child, femur fractured, angel-razed.
       greed—unfolding you with perhaps;
& perhaps, here, face sheared, facing this gulf,
       we, ascension through all meat,

       but here, & corruption sounds meat;
a separate love sounds void's solar sylphs,
       we, extinction with mouths;
the Pyrrhic blooms as song aligns to meat,
       the we-architects under summer's thunder,
organ's arbors washed through with hallowed filth;
       summer's white fractured by scythe,
hand in hand, lawless hearts heartless, we feast,
       our arbors sheared, no scarred genocide

       cleansing.
we mouths remain for all corruption, our

summer's greed, lust spent for scab, wine, & scar.

ix.

      & America enfolds
Donna, would the root be also the pit,
      we skies, people.
the stem also crown for inner arbors?
      Our plumes, must people,
Do we crease the leaves grown mist prophetic,
      not specified stems;
eyes that "I" claim saw the shoot's green ardor
      we empty American

      stretch speech-harvests;
before the fig's heart flowers, the center
      empty-hearted,
through which we the we-wasp feasts? We condone
      empty death, our strips enfold—
madness, ravenous, we drink dry, render
      we rag roots & sovereign states—
blind in blight the root as both stem & stone:
      sovereign for strangling,

      blight quill, sovereign sun,
the weed the *we* strangling the known. Alone,
      higher melt, principle our sores,
we are not—for we seed the desert for
      alone, not states—homelands;
forest, the forest for quill, the quill's prone
      Donna loves Donna
pride, our eye's core opens as our sun sores
      homogeneous; white core,

      we rag our purpose crushed Constitution,
to melt the soft wax of our wing as we
      rag our latest pulp Donna,
fly o'er the holy waste our love's fall feeds.
      & rag our wings for ceaseless skies.

PERSONAL EFFECTS, RICHARD VALENZUELA

found on body at scene of death

1 silver crucifix & religious medal

Brown leather pocket case with black lacing & stamped design

Numerous miscellaneous receipts

Several photos

Cash $22.15 less $11.65 coroner's fees—$10.50

Check on Hollywood office, California bank, 1600 N. Vine St., Hollywood, Calif. #359

$50.00 (noted—advance as per contract)

Check, same as above, #360, $50.00 (noted—advance as per contract)

Bracelet silver chain with DONNA attached.

[IF YOU THINK]

If you think
            this is a
                        book of "sad,"

think again.
            Thank again.
                        These pages

are my hands,
            you're holding
                        my hands:

lift me up
            like I'm new-
                        born, like a

ballerina,
            & spin me;
                        you've made two

more dreams come
            true; remem-
                        ber, sorrow

is also proof
            of our joy

                        to

            survive.

ACKNOWLEDGMENTS

GRATITUDE to the four directions, to the four elements, to the earth, to the air, to fire and water, to the seen and to the unseen, to you and your eyes on this page, to the ancestors, to the land on which this book was written, San Jose, California, to recognize this land's continued importance to the indigenous Muwekma Ohlone people.

The author is deeply grateful to the editors of *Anne Carson: Ecstatic Lyre* from University of Michigan Press, *Kweli Journal, Visible Binary, Cloud Rodeo*, and *Eleven Eleven* for featuring earlier versions of these writings.

Endless thanks to Penguin editor Paul Slovak for his patience, dedication, insight, wisdom, and trust. Great thanks to the graphic design team at Penguin for their wonderful talent, patience, trust, and compassion. Penguin Books, my deepest gratitude.

Great thanks to my friends and family for their support: Jeffrey Pethybridge, Carolina Ebeid & Patrick Pethybridge—endless friendship & gratitude; Andrea Rexilius & Eric Baus; Rosebud Ben-Oni, Mathias Svalina, Vincent Toro & Grisel Acosta, Matthew Thomas, Peggy Yocom, Jerry & Mary Martinez, Mark Martinez, Ivan Martinez, Tiffany Martinez, Dante Martinez, Talia Martinez, Tyler Martinez, Trinity Martinez. Dan Beachy-Quick for his generous words. Roberto Tejada, you are an inspiration.

Carmen Giménez—my dear friend, thank you & I love you.

Teresa Rosa Veramendi—you, my light ever swiftly.

A very special thank-you to: Angelspit & the art of mixtapes; these companions & teachers, sonic lovers & compassionate friends, our music's elevating, translating & continuously rendering the joyful vibrance as this raw no-you all-awe now: Ritchie Valens, My Bloody Valentine, Dead Prez, Depeche Mode, Nine Inch Nails, Björk, Deftones, Saul Williams, the Delfonics, the Jackson 5, Lonelyspeck, Smashing Pumpkins, Max Richter, Boy in Static, Placebo, Bon Jovi, Black Sheep, the Cure, Miguel, the Supremes, Moto Boy, Michael Franti, the Editors, Pictureplane, Ice Cube, New Order, Placebo, Rage Against the Machine, Ani DiFranco, Catherine

Wheel, Tracy Chapman, Wolf Club, Finch, Tegan and Sara, Sarah McLachlan, Health, Sombear, BT, PJ Harvey, Tori Amos, the Four Tops, Rise Against, Chevelle, Jeff Buckley, Kent, Lifehouse, My Vitriol, Ride, Spotlights, Sigur Rós & so many more . . .

NOTES

AN ANGELLO FABRICATION

A riff on Aaron Angello's wonderful methodology in *The Fact of Memory* (Rose Metal
Press), wherein he writes creative nonfiction meditations on each word of Shake-
speare's Sonnet 29; his book performs what Elisa Gabbert describes as "a kind of
fractal memoir." Here, I wrote, meditating on each word of the chorus of Ritchie
Valens's "We Belong Together."

ARBOLES DE LA VIDA

Sam Slote, "Thoroughly Modern Modernism: Modernism and Its Postmodernisms," in
Modernism, eds. Astradur Eysteinsson and Vivian Liska (Amsterdam: John Benja-
mins Publishing Company, 2007), 233–49.

LETTERS TO RITCHIE

Letter III

Allen Grossman with Mark Halliday, *The Sighted Singer* (Baltimore: Johns Hopkins
University Press, 1991), 265.

Letter VIII

Ken Kelley, "Luis Valdez: The Interview," *San Francisco Focus*, September 1987, 104–5.
David Savran, "Border Tactics: Luis Valdez Distills the Chicano Experience on Stage
and Film," *American Theatre*, January 1988, 20.

Letter XV

Mariana Castillo Deball, *Ixiptla* (Berlin, Germany: Bom Dia Boa Tarde Boa Noite,
2014), printedmatter.org/catalog/39914.
Boaventura de Sousa Santos, *The End of the Cognitive Empire: The Coming of Age of Episte-
mologies of the South* (Durham, North Carolina: Duke University Press, 2018), 3.

Letter XVII

Walter Benjamin, *Illuminations*, ed. Hannah Arendt, trans. Harry Zohn (New York:
Schocken, 1969), 257–58.
Angel Dominguez, "A Backyard Funeral Afterparty para Latinidad," *Open Space*, San
Francisco Museum of Modern Art, November 5, 2021, openspace.sfmoma.org
/2021/11/a-backyard-funeral-afterparty-para-latinidad.

Letter XVIII

Micaela Díaz-Sánchez and Alexandro D. Hernández, "The *Son Jarocho* as Afro-Mexican Resistance Music," *Journal of Pan African Studies* 6, no. 1 (July 2013): 187–209.

Boaventura de Sousa Santos, *Epistemologies of the South: Justice Against Epistemicide* (New York: Routledge, 2016), 171–72.

Letter XXI

Friedrich Hölderlin, *The Death of Empedocles: A Mourning-Play*, trans. by David Farrell Krell (Albany: State University of New York Press, 2008).

G. S. Kirk and J. E. Raven, *The Presocratic Philosophers* (New York: Cambridge University Press, 1957), 327.

A more literal analogy could be found in Roger Caillois's classic essay "Mimicry and Legendary Psychasthenia," where an insect, in mimicking plant life, disappears so completely into its environment, the mimicry so complete, others of its ilk feed upon it as if it were the plant. Thus, dispossessed of those aesthetic distinctions defining it, the insect's aesthetic mimicry becomes the natural &, in being cannibalized, its very undoing.

THE DONNA SONNETS [INFECTED TEXT]

Shawn Hubler, Thomas Fuller, Anjali Singhvi, and Juliette Love, "Many Latinos Couldn't Stay Home. Now Virus Cases Are Soaring in Their Communities," *The New York Times*, June 26, 2020.

Tom Mirovski, "How to Make a Nature Poem," bax.site.wesleyan.edu/bax-2016/tom -mirovski.

Allen Grossman with Mark Halliday, *The Sighted Singer* (Baltimore: Johns Hopkins University Press, 1991), 256.

TERESA VERAMENDI

J. MICHAEL MARTINEZ is the author of three collections of poetry, including *Heredities*, which received the Walt Whitman Award from the Academy of American Poets, and *Museum of the Americas*, which was a winner of the National Poetry Series Competition and long-listed for the 2018 National Book Award for Poetry. He is an assistant professor in the Department of English and Comparative Literature at San José State University.

PENGUIN POETS